The Humble Essay
Third Edition

Roy K. Humble

Problem Child Press
Dallas, Oregon

The Humble Essay, Third Edition
Copyright © 2015. All rights reserved.
Problem Child Press • problemchildpress.com

ISBN: 978-0-9818181-9-1, 0981818196

Cover photograph © 2007 by Samuel Richardson. Used by permission.

Printed in the United States of America.

Contents

Introduction
Anyone Can Learn How to Write

A lot of student writers don't seem to be very happy about being student writers. When they get a paper assignment, they ignore it for as long as possible — until roughly eleven o'clock on the night before it's due. And then they simply start typing, hoping with all their hearts that whatever comes out of their fingertips will not need to be revised.

Is this your own sad story, student writer?

There are usually two reasons for this kind of procrastination. One reason, I'm sad to say, is laziness. Some people just trend toward lazy. And remarkably, lazy has somehow worked for them in the past. *The Humble Essay* won't help anyone be less lazy. Only life can teach you that — as it will, and probably with something a little more devastating than lousy grades. But the other reason for procrastination is pain avoidance, and if pain is why you put off writing, *The Humble Essay* can help.

With college writing, the pain you are trying to avoid comes mostly from not knowing what you're doing. You have to guess about what to do, which is frustrating by itself, but worse is knowing that every guess you make has a good chance of lowering your grade. It's like having to dance in front of your girlfriend's sisters when 1) you already know you're a lousy dancer and 2) you also know that your girlfriend's sisters are comparing you to the previous boyfriend, the one with all the hair. And the dimples.

But the simple and encouraging truth about college writing is that it's just a thing you do. If you can figure out how to drive a car or take care of a cat or manipulate loved ones into doing the dishes for you — and you can — then you can figure out how to write a college essay. It's not that complicated. You just have to take the learning process seriously.

To get started, you need to have a better understanding of what's expected of you. That's where *The Humble Essay* comes in. The first half of

1

this book explains what the college essay is and how formal writing differs from the informal writing you're used to. It lays out what's expected of you so that you can stop guessing about that. The second half of the book shows you how to put these guidelines into practice so that the essays you create will meet those formal expectations. You still have to read the book carefully — this isn't a vampire novel, after all — but you can handle that. In fact, it's a good idea for you to read every chapter twice. The second time through is where you do most of the learning, believe it or not.

> **"Learning how to write the college essay is a lot like learning how to French kiss. Reading about it will only take you so far."**

To start putting these ideas into practice, it's also a good idea to work with someone who is more experienced at writing than you are, someone who can help you understand these ideas and check your progress. If you're reading this book because a writing professor has forced you to read it, then you're in luck. Make good use of that professor. Go to her office hours with questions. Raise your hand in class and ask her what she means by "discourse community." Read — twice — every comment on every paper. Many schools offer free tutoring from writing teachers or accomplished students, and that's another excellent source of help. Don't be shy about getting extra help whenever you need it. That's why it's there, after all.

To really know what you're doing, however, the main thing you have to do is simply write, and write a lot, so that you can see for yourself what it means to put these ideas into practice. Learning how to write the college essay is a lot like learning how to French kiss. Reading about it will only take you so far. To really learn how to do it, you have to actually do it — again and again and again.

Don't be afraid of struggling. You *will* struggle. So what? Whenever you learn to do something new — roller-skating, computer programming, darts, *anything* — making mistakes is an important part of the learning process. In fact, it shows that you're getting somewhere. So don't take those mistakes personally. You certainly can't look at them as failures. You just have to make your mistakes, correct them, and then move on to more sophisticated errors. Mistakes are not a big deal.

One day in first grade, I got a frowny face on a math test. My class had moved from addition to subtraction without any warning, and I'd missed seven of nine problems. Seven of nine! I was a mess the rest of the day, barely able to hold it together during the longest afternoon recess of my life.

When I came home from school, my mother was in her bedroom watching *Queen for a Day*, so I wasn't allowed to bother her, but my big sister Nadine was in the living room practicing for her interpretive dance recital. I dropped onto the couch and began crying.

"What now?" she said.

I blubbered to her about the frowny face.

"Well," she said, gently waving her arms like a willow tree enlivened by a summer breeze. "It's just *math*. Even a dodo bird can learn *math*."

That was one of the most supportive things Nadine ever said to me. It gave me the courage to return to school the next day and begin the hard work of learning how to subtract. And she was right, too. It was just math, and with enough practice — and just a little help — any dodo bird really *can* learn how to do math.

Learning how to write the college essay might be a little painful for a while. It might not be the first thing you want to do on a Friday night — or Wednesday morning. But student writer, always remember that it's just writing. It's just the college essay. You don't need to dread it or avoid it any longer. You just need to acquire a few basic ideas. You need to put them into practice. And in no time at all, you'll find that it's easy enough to keep writing because the guessing will be over. You'll know what you're doing.

Part One

The College Essay Is Something You Make

Part One Overview

The Form of Formal Writing

Most of the writing that you have done up until now is called **informal writing**. Informal writing is like talking. It doesn't have to follow many rules. It just has to make sense. This is how you've written almost everything so far, including school papers. Your high school and middle school teachers may have called those papers "essays," which suggests they were formal papers, but most of the time they were more like conversations. You wrote down the words that you would otherwise have spoken.

Informal writing is great for informal situations — e-mails, texts, letters written on actual paper to elderly relatives — because in those situations, your ideas don't matter that much. What matters is the personal connection that your words create between you and your readers. Think about those two-hour phone conversations you used to have with the people who eventually outgrew you. It didn't matter what you talked about — "You hang up!" "No, you hang up!" What mattered was that you were joined together in those sweet moments that are now somewhat embarrassing memories.

Even when you wrote school papers, what you had to say wasn't as important as how well you said it. If you had a way with words, your papers were fun for teachers to read, and you got good grades. Meanwhile, if you were among the majority of students who *weren't* able to charm their teachers with lovely fluff, then no matter how great your ideas were, you got Cs for your obviously painful efforts. But those days are gone forever, student writer. Over and done with. With college writing, what matters is not a personal connection but having something worthwhile to say.

College writing is called **formal writing** because it has to have a certain shape or — wait for it — form. That form is defined by all sorts of rules. You have rules about how paragraphs should be structured, rules about how sentences should be shaped and punctuated, rules about how papers should be formatted, rules about how to give credit to others when you borrow their ideas or words. Rules upon rules that define what your formal readers expect from you.

These expectations make it hard to write how you talk because your paper has to be like everyone else's paper. Your only option is to adopt that prescribed form. Otherwise, you'll stand out like a doofus. And even if fitting in is painful at first for you former stars of the informal paper, fitting in is still a good thing. It means that anyone can be heard and understood. You don't have to have a way with words anymore. You just have to follow these rules so that your paper looks like every other formal paper. That uniformity allows your ideas to stand on their own.

This is important in college because your professors are constantly checking to see what's going on inside your brain. They rely on the rules of formal writing to strip away your charming personality so they can see your ideas. And formal writing is even more important after college. Formal writing is how people communicate in court, government, business, and the rest of the professional world. If you want your ideas to be understood and respected, you have to learn the rules for formal writing and put them into practice. You have to show your formal readers that you know how to play this particular game.

In this first half of this book, we'll focus on the essay as a thing that you create — a form of writing. We'll look at the purpose of the essay and how it's usually different from the purpose of informal writing. We'll look at formal and informal paragraphs. We'll spend two chapters looking at sentences, where the rules of formal writing are the most technical and precise.

Take your time with these chapters — especially the more technical ones. If something seems boring, that's probably because it doesn't make sense yet. So read it again. If it still doesn't make sense, then suck it up and ask your professor about it. The more time you invest in learning these rules, the sooner you'll be able to follow them confidently. The sooner you get comfortable with this form of writing, the more you'll be able to focus on educating yourself about new topics and developing great ideas.

That's when the real fun begins.

Chapter 1
The College Essay Is Your Own Idea

The purpose of the college essay — like the purpose of almost all formal writing — is to explain one opinion of your own.

We often use that word "opinion" as a synonym for "guess" or "hunch." That's not the sort of opinion we're talking about here. For a college essay, the main idea must be a *reasonable* opinion, an idea based on thoughtful consideration of relevant information.

I wish it were more complicated so that I could explain it to you more impressively, but it really is that simple. Or it would be that simple if so many of your teachers hadn't confused the issue by playing fast and loose with the word "essay." Since grade school, you've heard this word used to describe just about anything made with sentences. Your English teachers haven't helped matters by tossing around technical terms as if you under-stood them — or cared. So before we move on to the important work of learning how to write the college essay, we'll start by clearing up some common misunderstandings.

Commonly Misunderstood Terms

The first thing we need to do need is untangle three important terms that will be used to explain how essays work — **thesis**, **thesis statement**, and **topic**. This won't take too long, but you do have to think about it. You can't skim. And this *will* be on the midterm.

Thesis and Thesis Statement

The word "thesis" is a Greek term that means "proposal" or "assertion." When talking about college essays, thesis means "your main idea." English teachers like to use "thesis" in place of "main idea" because it's a Greek word,

9

and there's something about Greek words that make English teachers purr with contentment.

As long as you understand that "thesis" means "main idea," those Greek-loving English teachers won't pose a serious problem for you. However, keep in mind that the thesis of an essay is not the same as the "thesis statement." The thesis is your idea, your opinion, a fleeting bit of electrochemical activity inside your brain. The thesis *statement* is a single, written sentence that states your thesis. See how that works? It translates the intangible idea that lives in your brain into tangible words on an actual piece of paper or computer screen.

Here's a table, for those who like tables:

Thesis and Thesis Statement

	Thesis	*Thesis Statement*
Definition	An assertion, the main idea of an essay	A written sentence that articulates a thesis into actual words
Key Quality	Exists only as an idea — intangible	Exists only as written words, a sentence — tangible

The distinction between "thesis" and "thesis statement" seems easy enough, but a few rogue English teachers confuse this as well by using "thesis" for both your main idea and the written sentence that defines your main idea. With these teachers, pay attention to how they use "thesis" in a sentence. If they ask *what* your thesis is, they mean, "What's your main idea?" If they ask *where* your thesis is, they mean, "Where in your essay have you hidden a one-sentence summary of your main idea? Because I'll be honest with you, student writer, I can't find it. Not anywhere."

For an essay to really be an essay, by the way, it needs to have a thesis, not just a thesis statement. It's a good idea to put a thesis statement in your essay, of course. It tells your readers what your thesis is, and that's a helpful hint for them. But by itself, a thesis statement doesn't turn your paper into an essay. For it to be an essay, all of your paragraphs must collectively present a single main idea of your own — your thesis.

Thesis and Topic

Some student writers have developed the habit of using "topic" and "thesis" interchangeably. This isn't surprising. "Topic" is a vague term, just like "thesis," and the term "topic sentence" refers to a sentence that states the main idea of a paragraph — the same thing that a thesis statement does for a whole essay. The similarity between "topic sentence" and "thesis statement" makes "topic" seem a lot like "thesis."

However, "topic" and "thesis" don't mean the same thing. The topic is the subject of the essay, the thing about which you have an opinion — a poem you read, a scientific theory you studied, the life cycle of nematodes, or anything else that your professor told you to study and write about. The thesis of an essay is your reasonable opinion about that topic.

Perhaps this table will help explain things:

Topic, Thesis, and Thesis Statement

	Topic	Thesis	Thesis Statement
Definition	The subject of an essay	The main idea of an essay	A written sentence that articulates the thesis
Example	Deer	The idea about deer that is explained by my essay	Deer are dangerous animals.
Example	Voting requirements	The idea about voting requirements that is explained by my essay	Voters should have to accurately describe what they're voting for before they can vote.
Example	The ending of "A Good Man is Hard to Find," by Flannery O'Connor	The idea I have about the ending that is explained by my essay	The ending of O'Connor's story teaches us how unsafe it is to reach out and touch someone.

The Topic, Thesis, and Thesis Statement at Work

Now let's look at how these three terms apply to the process of writing an essay. The topic of your essay is the subject that you are writing about — a thing of some sort — a person, a theory about time, the mating habits of tree frogs, petroglyphs. It was probably assigned to you, or if it wasn't assigned, then you were given some boundaries and asked to pick a subject for yourself from within those boundaries. Having a topic is the usual starting point of the writing process.

The next step is to study this topic, exploring and considering information about it. If it's a poem, for example, you read that poem about a hundred times, trying to figure out why in the world *anyone* would write a poem about a shopping list and how good plums taste. Who cares how plums taste? You read what others have to say about it. You complain to your professor and ask him to assign Edgar Allen Poe next time. Gradually, and in spite of your distaste for this poem, your self-education still leads you to certain conclusions of your own, opinions about the meaning of this poem, how good it is or isn't, the importance of plums, and so on. You then pick one of those opinions to write about. That opinion becomes the thesis of your essay.

When you write your essay, you focus entirely on your thesis — your own, somewhat reasonable opinion that the plums symbolize sex and death. In the opening paragraph, you introduce the poem and its poet. Then, because you can't explain everything in the poem, you present your focus within the poem — the meaning of the plums. Finally, you present your main idea about those plums in a single sentence, your thesis statement: "The plums represent sex and death."

In the body of the essay, you present evidence from what others say that will help you explain and defend your thesis. You list the objections some might have to your thesis and then you respond to each objection — politely, of course. For a few minutes you are tempted to add a juicy fact you uncovered about the poet's rather bizarre private life, but then you wisely say to yourself, "No. I can't go there. I must not. This has nothing to do with my thesis." And when all this has been presented, you wrap things up by summarizing the evidence in the body and restating your main idea.

The College Essay and What It Is Not

Now that those three terms are clear in your mind, we'll move on to the most misunderstood term of them all, "essay." According to your teachers, you've been writing "essays" since the first day of third grade when beloved Mrs. Webster asked the class to write an essay about your summer vacation. Since then, you've written hundreds of "essays" that were actually stories, reports, reflection papers, and other types of writing — but not essays. To undo those long years of misunderstanding, we'll look at some of the non-essays from your past and compare them to the college essay. With each example, notice how the difference always comes back to whether or not its purpose is to present your own main idea.

College Essays vs. Stories

A story recounts events, real or imagined. Stories are usually organized chronologically, and they tend to focus on the actions of their characters and how those actions usually lead to dire consequences. Stories engage readers because we're all suckers for finding out what happens next. We hope it will be something bad — for a while — and then that it will all work out for the best.

For storytelling to be effective within an essay, however, you can't just present the series of events. You must use those events to explain a main idea. If you don't have a main idea to explain, then the story remains just a story.

Here's an example of that:

> On the first night of our backpacking trip, Denise and I camped beside the river we'd followed upstream. We set up our tent on a small, sandy gravel bar to take advantage of the smooth ground and the soothing sound of the river. It was a beautiful campsite.
>
> By the time we'd eaten, it was already getting dark, so Denise said we should leave the dishes for the morning. We took a few minutes to watch the stars come out, and then we hit the sack. Denise was asleep instantly.
>
> It took me longer to fall asleep. Something didn't feel right. After perhaps an hour, I went outside to relieve myself. The stars had disappeared,

but I didn't think anything of it. I went back to bed and finally fell asleep. Later that night, I woke to the sound of light rain on the tent. Like the river, it was a peaceful sound, and it lulled me back to sleep. The next time I woke, it was from Denise jabbing me with her elbow.

"Wake up!" she shouted. "We're soaked!"

We were more than soaked. It was raining heavily. The rising river had swamped our tent, washed our cooking gear downstream, and drenched our food. Scrambling in the pre-dawn darkness, we were lucky to get our tent, packs, and sleeping bags up to higher ground. We found most of the cooking gear later that day, but the food — and the trip — were ruined.

In this example, the story might be used to illustrate several opinions, but the writer never actually presents an opinion or explains how the story illustrates that opinion. Because no main idea is presented or even implied, the story remains just a story. But here's an example of how this same experience could illustrate the main idea of an essay:

Whenever you go backpacking, the first rule is to respect the place you're traveling through. If you don't know this rule at the beginning of your backpacking trip, the place itself will be glad to teach it to you. That's what happened to my former girlfriend and me last summer. It was our first backpacking trip together, and, perhaps because she wanted to impress me, Denise acted as if she were in control of everything — including the weather and the river.

On our first night out, I wanted to set up camp about thirty feet back from the river so we wouldn't have to worry about rising water during the night. Denise laughed at my suggestion and set up our tent at the water's edge. She left our cooking gear and food on the gravel beside the tent.

That night, however, it rained. It only rained lightly at our campsite, but upstream it rained heavily, and the river rose almost four inches before we woke. By then, our cooking gear was a hundred yards downstream and our food was soaked. Denise tried to laugh as if it was no big deal, but the fact is we could have been drowned in our sleep. And even though we escaped death, it took most of the day to recover the gear and dry things out.

This was a disappointing trip, but it taught me a lesson that has guided me ever since: Respect the environment or the environment will make you respect it. This is true when camping beside the river, but it's also true at home, at school, or driving down the street where you live. You should never assume you're in control of the world around you.

The writer now does more than just present the event. He uses the story to illustrate and validate his thesis that you must respect your surroundings. The main idea is now the star of the show, and the story has shifted to a supporting role. Because of this shift in purpose, we have an essay instead of a story.

Here's a table, in case you were expecting one:

College Essay vs. Story

	Story	*Essay*
Topic	A backpacking mishap	Respecting your environment
Main Idea (as a thesis statement)	None	You should respect your environment.
Explanation	The details of the story help readers understand the topic (a mishap) rather than an idea about the topic.	The details of the story explain why this piece of advice is a reasonable idea.

Autobiography is one type of storytelling that sometimes looks like an essay but still isn't. With autobiography, the writer writes about the writer: My life has always been difficult. Moving to Omaha is the best thing that ever happened to me. Nobody understands me like my cats. And so on. If the writer presents one main opinion about himself or herself, then technically, I suppose, it's an essay. However, it's not much of an essay for two reasons. First, it's hard to say whether this is an opinion or a fact. No one can climb into the mind of the writer and argue that no, you know very well that your uncle Jimmy understands you much better than your cat(s). Second, and more importantly, the topic (me, me, me!) isn't relevant to your college classes. College classes tend to focus on something other than the students who take them.

This second reason brings us back to that distinction between informal and formal writing. Informal writing is usually personal, something that comes directly from the writer to the reader. When you wrote about your summer vacation, for example, you were building a bridge between you and beloved Mrs. Webster. You were sharing your summer experiences of riding bikes, going to the library, and falling out of your treehouse so that Mrs. Webster could share those experiences with you and know what was going on all summer while she sat quietly in her classroom waiting for school to resume.

College writing isn't personal in this way. It doesn't focus on you — or your reader — but on a topic that you and your reader have in common. For your a college audience, it doesn't matter that you got rained out while hiking. What matters is the topic of respecting the environment, a topic that you have in common with them. If you can illustrate that idea with personal experience, then okay, use personal experience. But if you really want to convince your reader about the validity of your idea, then you better do some research and see what others have to say, too.

In spite of everything I just said, autobiography can still be used effectively within an essay. Personal experiences draw readers into an essay, particularly if you come across as likable, someone the readers can relate to, and if the personal experience is relevant to your main idea. You just need to keep the autobiography in an appropriately minor, supporting role.

College Essays vs. Reports

Reports give readers information about a topic. They are common in elementary school and high school because they require students to educate themselves about a topic, and this gives them both new information and some practice with self-education, which is a valuable skill. Reports continue in college, too, and for the same reasons. They are also a common type of formal writing in many professional trades — human services, building inspection, fire and paramedic services — because so many trades require accurate observation and recording of information.

Reports aren't essays, however, because they don't provide readers with the writer's own opinion about the topic. In fact, it's fairly easy to write a perfectly acceptable report without thinking at all, as you may know from experience. Think of the times when you simply opened a book and copied down the information "in your own words" without letting it penetrate your brain. Think of the times when you scoured the Internet for the first website that had any information on your topic. Here's a typical report:

> According to Wikipedia, pigdogs live in packs of six to eight animals in established territories of up to one square mile. The territory tends to be bounded by natural features, such as rivers, or by man-made features, such as interstate highways or fences. The territory includes a year-round source of water and a shaded area known as the "sty" where the pigdogs lounge as often as they are able and occasionally yip in their sleep.
>
> Pigdogs first arrived in California as pets on a Norwegian freighter, the *Ibsen*, which docked in Sacramento in 1911. Having been thrown overboard by the sailors, the pigdogs swam to shore and soon flourished in the surrounding environment.
>
> Pigdogs run in packs of five to eight animals over small territories (often defined by roads or irrigation ditches). Females bear one litter of seven or eight pigpups every other year, except in times of drought. During times of drought, the females typically band together and fight off any rutting males, sometimes ferociously.
>
> The males are the hunters of the pack, although they will retreat from any animal that moves quickly, such as a rabbit or vole. Often they come back to the pack bearing fast-food wrappers and Pepsi cups or road kill that is not too intimidating. They may also stalk fruit and vegetables, acting as if the plants were dangerous animals, and bring these spoils back to the sty with great displays of pride.

In this example, the writer provides information that informs you about the topic of pigdogs. Because that information is the only thing that the writer offers, this is a report. For it to become an essay, the writer needs to present his or her own opinion about the significance of this information and then use the information to explain why that opinion makes sense.

Here's an example of an essay that uses the information about pigdogs to explain and defend the writer's thesis:

> Non-native species have a way of destroying the environments they invade, and that's why the California Department of Fish and Wildlife must act more aggressively in its attempts to eradicate this species. A good illustration of failed eradication can be found in the case of the Norwegian pigdogs that have taken over large parts of California's Central Valley, according to a study that was reported by Al Tobey (2014) in *Scientific Californian*.

Perhaps because they seem timid, or because of their odd habit of gathering roadside garbage, pigdogs have been considered harmless for decades (Bone 2011). It was only recently that wildlife biologists observed that pigdogs had begun to crowd out native species such as raccoons (Brase 2013). Efforts to curb the spread of pigdogs by removing roadside garbage only resulted in pigdogs moving into farmers' fields and orchards where they began a population explosion that continues today (Tobey 2014).

If more aggressive eradication tactics such as trapping, shooting, poisoning had been taken earlier, pigdogs would not now be eating one-third of California's annual artichoke crop, among other things.

This writer uses much of the same information about pigdogs, but it's now used to present and defend a thesis, which is stated in the first sentence. Any of the original information that doesn't help to support that opinion has been dropped from the second example. The fact that pigdogs arrived on a Norwegian ship, for example, doesn't help explain the thesis, so out it goes. Other information — such as how pigdogs have crowded out raccoons — has been added because the thesis *does* require it.

Here's another table, just in case:

College Essay vs. Report

	Report	*Essay*
Topic	Pigdogs	Eradicating non-native species from California
Main Idea (as a thesis statement)	None	The California Department of Fish and Wildlife must act more aggressively to eradicate non-native species.
Explanation	Specific information helps readers better understand the topic of pigdogs.	The negative example of pigdog proliferation defends the idea that aggressive measures should be taken.

Paraphrasing is a type of report that will sometimes act like an essay. With paraphrasing, the writer is able to report someone else's opinion by putting that idea into his or her own words. While the presence of an opinion makes the piece of writing look like an essay, it remains a report because the main idea is not an idea that came from the writer's own brain.

Here's an example:

> When students complain that teachers have screamed profanities in the classroom, many parents' first response is to file an angry complaint with school administrators. However, according to *Detached Educator*, the newsletter of the Almost Retired Teachers Association (ARTA), that might not be the best approach.
>
> "An incident of screaming can admittedly cause temporary problems," says Steve Richardson, ARTA president, "but why make things worse by making a big deal about it?" According to Richardson, it's best to let the situation resolve itself over the course of several months, or even years.

You will regularly need to paraphrase the ideas of others. It's a good way to compress and include their ideas as you explain your own main idea. It just can't be a substitute for your own thinking.

College Essays vs. Reflection Papers

A reflection paper is a collection of *several* opinions or observations that are united only by their relevance to a given topic. The assignment is usually open-ended — explain your reactions to chapter 3, describe what you like about this article, and so on. Teachers often assign reflection papers to compel you to actually read and maybe think about the assigned reading. Why you wouldn't do the reading on your own is a mystery to your professors, but they embrace that mystery by assigning these free-form reflection papers. However, even if a reflection paper is assigned by a college professor, it's not an essay because it doesn't focus on just one main idea.

Reflection papers are almost always informal rather than formal. Two things make them informal. First, they focus on you, the writer. They gather up a collection of your observations, your experiences, your guesses, and your ideas. Second, the form of the paper doesn't usually matter. You just need to record your experience of reading or viewing or of pretending to read or view the assigned topic. You put things down in whatever order you think of them. With formal writing, the focus must stay on the shared topic and provide information about the shared topic. Sometimes that information comes from personal experience, but more often it comes from studying the topic itself.

You often find reflection papers in the letters-to-the-editor section of the local newspaper. Someone gets steamed about the way teachers have summers off or how baseball players shouldn't wear baggy pants — or whatever — and they respond by typing angrily. What comes out of their fingertips seems coherent because it sticks to one topic and is unified by the same angry mood, but there's no single, main idea. What the writer is really doing is showing readers what he or she feels about that something. The writer's emotions become more important than whatever it was that stirred them up. There's no attempt to present and defend a single opinion about that topic.

With college writing, an essay assignment can easily turn into a reflection paper when the student writer either can't decide what to focus on or is unwilling to take a stand on just one position. Instead, the writer writes circles around a topic and hopes that it will miraculously become an essay. Occasionally this does generate a miracle, but don't be encouraged by that.

Here's an example of a typical reflection paper:

> Writing is very important. You have to be able to write in order to succeed in our society. People expect you to write well. If you can't express yourself well as a writer, then you will miss out on many important opportunities.
>
> The use of writing has been with us for thousands of years, but in the past only the elite needed to write. Since the invention of the printing press, however, writing has become more important with each passing year until now almost everyone needs to write. Nowadays, with the arrival of computers and e-mail and texting, writing is even more essential to the world in which we live.
>
> It isn't easy to learn to be a good writer, but a good teacher can help you to gain the skills that will make you a better writer. You will find that with stronger skills, you have much more confidence, and confidence translates into success!

If you're assigned to write a reflection paper about a topic, then reflect all you want. Add lots of opinions. Let your hair down, if you have hair to let down. However, if you're assigned to write an essay, you need to be disciplined and make sure it doesn't turn into a reflection paper.

One way to prevent a reflection paper from happening is to resist the urge to simply vent your emotions. Emotions are fine, but they aren't the same as thinking. It's not sufficient to "feel strongly" about a topic. You must instead *think* strongly. Second, take some time to actually figure out what you think about a topic. Do that before you start writing your essay. Don't start putting words onto the page and expect that somehow a single opinion will emerge or that, in the absence of an idea, your professor will be impressed by your use of many fine, long words. With your friends, you might call that sort of writing "B.S." Your professors have other and worse names for it.

When you choose to simply vent or B.S. about a topic, what you're really doing is choosing to not educate yourself about that topic. You're going with what you already know or feel. You haven't taken the time to find some new idea that wasn't already in your heart or brain. I don't want to make you feel bad about yourself, student writer, but you're wasting a perfectly good opportunity to make yourself smarter. Here is one example of how the writer could narrow the paper's focus and, with some self-education, develop at a more interesting thesis for an essay:

> In a recent *People* magazine poll, 59 percent of the respondents said that writing freaked them out. On a recent television reality show, only one of six participants was willing to write a typical college-level essay, even when offered a hundred dollars. The problem? People feel inadequate about their writing skills. But that all seems to be changing, thanks to the Internet. To use the Internet, you have to read, and you have to write.
>
> Most of that reading and writing happens when Internet users send, receive, and respond to e-mail. Many online games require less formal writing, but they require more of it and at a faster pace. Using websites as a source of information doesn't require the same level of writing, but social networking sites such as Facebook use writing extensively.
>
> Even though many users may not be aware of how much writing they are doing, the writing still has its impact. Internet users, whether they realize it or not, are becoming more and more comfortable with the written word.
>
> According to Dr. Jerry Trabue of the Eastern Central University of Northern Kentucky, it all comes down to classical conditioning. Writing within a more comfortable environment helps writers to associate that feeling of comfort

with the writing itself. And that makes them feel more adequate as writers. He notes that while 59 percent of *People* magazine readers are still freaked out about writing, that number is down from 63 percent two years ago.

So while the growing use of the Internet makes writing more important, that growing importance does not seem to be making people more uncomfortable with writing. Instead, it seems to be helping them become more confident and prolific writers.

In this version, the writer stays focused on just one reasonable opinion about writing, and each paragraph has a clear connection to that thesis. The opening paragraph introduces the topic and main idea. The next paragraph illustrates how much writing happens on the Internet. Then there's a transition, and the next paragraphs explain how all that writing may change how people feel about their writing skills. The last paragraph summarizes the explanation provided by the body of the essay and, in doing so, again emphasizes the main idea. And notice, too, that the information comes from studying the topic itself, not from personal experience. Kudos, student writer!

Here is another table that may or may not help:

College Essay vs. Reflection Paper

	Reflection Paper	**Essay**
Topic	The importance of writing	Impact of increased Internet use on attitudes toward writing
Main Idea (as a thesis statement)	There is no main idea. Each paragraph contains one or more different ideas about the topic.	The increased use of the Internet seems to be making people more confident writers because it requires so much writing.
Explanation	Because the essay skips from idea to idea, no single idea is illustrated with more than a broad and passing summary of information.	Paragraph 2 illustrates the increased amounts of writing required. Paragraphs 3 and 4 explain how attitudes are changing among Internet users.

College Essays and Five-Paragraph Trainer-Essays

The "essay" that you wrote in high school was probably a five-paragraph trainer-essay. The five-paragraph trainer-essay is to a real essay what a training bra is to a real bra. You feel like you've written a grown-up essay, and it certainly looks like one. However, it's almost never an actual, fully developed essay.

The five-paragraph trainer-essay is actually an organizational template. An introductory paragraph presents the topic and main idea. Each of three body paragraphs then covers one subtopic or idea about the main topic. A concluding paragraph restates the main idea and the point of each of the body paragraphs. You can insert anything into this template as long as it's related to the main topic. If you insert raw information into the body paragraphs, it becomes a five-paragraph report. If you insert a new opinion into each of the body paragraphs, it becomes a five-paragraph reflection paper.

The five-paragraph trainer-essay is easy for teachers to explain and easy for students to use. It's something a beginning writer can accomplish at an early age. In other words, your middle school and high school teachers were doing the right thing when they taught you and the other fledglings to use this template. That was a great starting point. It introduced you to the idea of making sure your writing has a certain shape.

The problem, though, is that an organizational template like this tends to generate essays that oversimplify and under-explain your thinking. That might be fine when you're young and don't have anything to say anyway, but with the college essay, your main idea is supposed to be thoughtful and complex. A thoughtful and complex idea has a hard time surviving in three body paragraphs.

Instead of forcing your thesis to squeeze into those three body paragraphs, you need to force your body paragraphs to increase and multiply until your thesis is fully explained. If a fully formed idea can be explained in five paragraphs, then fine, write a five-paragraph essay. So be it. But if your thesis is more complex and requires six or twelve or sixteen supporting paragraphs, then so be that. Set your five-paragraph trainer-essay aside and get on with the task of writing college essays.

Although the five-paragraph trainer-essay is in fact a type of formal writing — because it has to a certain shape — the complex ideas you write in college will require more complex forms than this. Most student writers seem willing to accept that concept. However, it's one thing to accept an idea, and it's another thing to put that idea into practice. Long years of practice have hard-wired it into your brain and probably your DNA. The five-paragraph trainer-essay is what you will write until you forcefully rip it from your brain and say, "No more!" That may sound a bit extreme, but that's what required. It will not go gently.

College Essays vs. Artful Essays

The college essay is not the only kind of essay out there. It will get the job done for most of your college writing, and it will do so effectively. However, it's not the sort of essay that you will find in respected magazines and over-priced college anthologies. It's not art, in other words.

Artful essays use more advanced methods to present their main ideas. The venerable E. B. White, for example, could write an essay about watching his son jump into a lake and, in sharing his simple observations, somehow unravel the mysteries of the life cycle. He did this with careful arrangement of images, with careful selection of words, and with only minor and understated discussion of his thesis. On the surface, it looks like a story or a reflection paper, but because of those advanced techniques, White still gets his thesis across to us.

These artful essays are usually informal. As in the case of E. B. White, they're often based entirely on personal experience and observation. You connect to the writer at a personal level. Because they're written for the broad readership of national magazines, they must engage and entertain readers so that they enjoy themselves and will hopefully renew their subscriptions.

If you didn't know any better, and if you already have a way with words, you might be tempted to skip over these sensible guidelines for writing the college essay and take on the challenge of writing your own artful essays. That desire to engage readers with personal stories and artful writing can be a strong temptation. I urge caution.

One problem with artful essays is that while they are easy to read, they are difficult to write. For most of us, they are out of reach while we're in college. Or while we're in grad school. Or while we're slogging through life teaching English composition for part-time wages at a community college in the middle of nowhere. For every E. B. White, there are another twenty thousand who think they are E. B. White.

The more important problem with artful essays, however, is that aside from a few young, untarnished English professors, your college professors aren't particularly interested in reading them. They want to see your ideas about the topics they've assigned, and they want to see your ideas explained clearly and concisely. They want more formal papers, in other words. They want college essays. They have dozens of other papers to read besides yours, too, so they will become ill-tempered if you stray from your assigned task in order to unravel the mysteries implicit in your recent journey to the refrigerator.

Don't lose heart over this, aspiring student writer. Wonderful, artful essays might indeed be part of your future. The odds are against it, but it could still happen. My uncle — true story — has been hit by lightning *twice*, so anything can happen. In the meantime, though, you have college essays to write — essays that are due next Thursday, or possibly tomorrow morning — and for these assignments, you should write the college essay that's introduced here. Don't work too hard to dazzle a professor with a stunningly artful informal paper when all that she or he really wants is a formal paper that presents a single good idea of your own.

The Other Purpose of the College Essay

So far in this chapter, you've seen that the purpose of the college essay is to present one idea of your own, to explain that idea clearly and defend it with sufficient, detailed evidence. That's what you give to your readers. However, there's a second purpose for the college essay, and that's what the essay gives to you as its writer.

Your professors don't assign you essays for their own benefit. They have plenty to do without requiring your essays to fill their evening hours with pleasure and delight. They only assign essays — at no small personal cost to themselves — because they want you to enjoy their academic disciplines the way that they enjoy their academic disciplines. Writing an essay allows you — and forces you — to see for yourself how that discipline works, to see what your professors do when they aren't teaching.

The word "essay" actually means "to explore." And that's what professors do when they're not teaching. They read about new topics. They follow their curiosity into deeper understandings of those topics. They snoop around libraries and hang out at field stations. They talk about these topics with their colleagues. They let their minds wander. They come up with all sorts of interesting questions and then poke around looking for information that will help them

> **"There is no such thing as a bad topic. Any topic — *every* topic — has something to offer if you look closely enough."**

to find a good answer. By assigning you that essay, they've essentially said, "Join me. This is *so cool.*"

So join them already. Don't write essays about topics you already understand. That's not exploring. Don't recycle old work you've turned in for other classes. That's not exploring, either. You've been there. You've done that. And for the love of all things academic and good, don't download or buy or borrow someone else's essay and pass it off as your own work. That's as bad for your soul as it is for your education — and by the way, it's also not exploring. When you do any of the above, you don't learn anything worthwhile. You don't let the essay give you anything. And you certainly don't develop an appreciation for what it means to explore within that discipline.

You might ask, "But how can I explore a topic that's boring?" Listen — it's boring because you haven't explored it yet. There is no such thing as a bad topic. Any topic — *every* topic — has something to offer if you look closely enough.

How do you explore a topic that seems at first glance to be boring? All you have to do is get started. Read about it. Talk to your professor about it. Find a reference librarian and ask for direction. If you will just take that first baby step, something will pop up that interests you, and then you can narrow your focus to explore that smaller part of the topic and really dig in. And that will be engaging and rewarding work. It won't be boring.

You might ask, "But how can I explore a topic I don't care about?" You don't care about it because you don't understand it. You don't understand it because you haven't explored it yet. It's a vicious cycle. The only way out is to just get started. The rest will follow. You'll end up with a new topic that you *do* care about.

You might ask a bunch of other questions, too — questions that are not really asking for information so much as defending you from having to do anything strenuous. I have the same basic answer to all of those questions — explore, explore, explore. It's that simple. I'm not kidding. Once you do that, you will enjoy the work ahead. The essays you write will give you treasures that outlast your grades by decades.

College is here to stretch you into something larger and more interesting than your current self. We've talked about this. You should be ready to not just accept but embrace assignments that require you to look at new topics. Don't run away from these apparently boring or difficult topics. Don't beg to write about something you already understand or care about. This momentary discomfort is a good thing. That's what you or your loved ones or *someone* is buying with all that tuition — new topics, new ideas, a new and improved version of you.

That's the second purpose of the essay — to give you something worth your while by encouraging you to explore new topics.

The Big Ideas

This chapter covered a lot of ground and introduced a few new terms. To help you organize all this new information, here are the big ideas from this chapter:

1. Terminology: To talk about how writing works, you have to use some technical terms. This chapter introduced the following technical terms:

- **topic:** the thing you are writing about — the price for a cup of coffee, for example.

- **thesis:** your own reasonable opinion about your topic — for example, the idea in your brain that a cup of coffee costs way too much.

- **thesis statement:** one sentence that defines your thesis — for example, words that you write down, such as, "A cup of coffee costs way too much."

2. The purpose of the college essay for readers: As a piece of formal writing, the purpose of the college essay is to provide your readers with your own main idea — to explain it and defend it. Unlike informal writing, its purpose is not to entertain your readers or build a connection between you and them. This purpose makes the college essay different from stories, reports, reflection papers, five-paragraph trainer-essays, and even an artful essay about that time you stuck your finger in an empty light socket and suddenly understood the true nature of electricity.

3. The purpose of the college essay for writers: With every writing assignment, remember that most of your professors don't assign you essays for their own benefit. They assign college essays so that you can see what it's like to do what they do — to explore their academic discipline, to educate themselves, to look at the world from that discipline's perspective, and to discover new ideas. So take that opportunity seriously. Every essay offers you another opportunity to be something more.

Chapter 2

The Essay Is Made of Paragraphs

Chapter 1 focuses on the purpose of the college essay and how it works one type of formal writing. In this and the chapters that follow, we take a much closer look at the form in formal writing. We start with paragraphs because paragraphs are the building blocks for just about any kind of formal paper.

A Brief Introduction to Formal Paragraphs

Because they have been writing informal papers all their lives, new college writers tend to start a new paragraph whenever they feel like it, and their feelings are guided not by the ideas within their essay but by appearances. They look at the page and see that they have accumulated four or five lines of text. This worries them. They don't want the paper to look boring, so they start a new paragraph.

Using paragraphs to make a paper look inviting is an old tradition, and that's mostly what you do with informal paragraphs. This is how paragraphs work whenever it's important to hold of the readers' attention — in newspapers, for example, or in popular magazines about celebrities going to the beach. Even in formal writing, it's not a terrible idea to occasionally divide a long paragraph into two logical pieces in order to make the page a little more inviting.

With formal writing, however, the main job for the paragraph is not to make the page look more inviting. What it has to do is to explain one smaller part of your essay. Paragraphs divide your essay into supporting ideas — reasons, examples, chunks of evidence — so that readers can look at each supporting piece carefully and then gradually see how those supporting ideas work together to explain and defend your main idea as a whole.

The reason to start a new formal paragraph is that you have a new idea or new chunk of information to explain. The reason to end a formal paragraph — no matter how long — is that the paragraph has fully presented that idea or chunk of information. With formal paragraphs, it's not about length anymore. You have to decide what each paragraph needs to explain, and then you have to take enough time to explain it clearly.

> **"With formal paragraphs, it's not about length anymore. You have to decide what each paragraph needs to explain, and then you have to take enough time to explain it clearly."**

The paragraphs in your essay come in three main groups — opening, body, and closing paragraphs. The opening paragraphs tell readers what to expect from the essay — the topic and the thesis and often what sort of evidence will be used. These paragraphs are like a map at the start of a trail that tells you where this particular trail will take you.

The body paragraphs then explain your essay's thesis by providing detailed information that shows what you mean by this idea and why your idea makes sense. Each paragraph is a section of trail that leads your readers from point A to point B to points C through W until they ultimately reach the final destination — an understanding of your thesis.

The closing paragraphs summarize the information from the body paragraphs and clarify how that information adds up to your thesis. These paragraphs are like a brief and surprisingly interesting slide show of the hike you just took. They look back fondly at the trail and remind your readers about where they traveled and where they ended up. These are nostalgic paragraphs that are mostly stuck in the past — not unlike your grandparents, who I'm sure are otherwise lovely people.

In the following pages, we'll look more closely at the work these different paragraphs do. To illustrate how this works, we'll use the actual paragraphs of a typical college essay.

Opening Paragraphs

Once you read the opening of a college essay, you should know what to expect from the rest of the essay. This is important with all types of formal writing because the professionals who read formal writing are not reading for pleasure. They're reading because it's part of their jobs. They need to know — right away — whether an essay or report or proposal will give them the information they need. They have no time to waste, so they want to know within a paragraph or two whether the essay or report has relevant information for them.

When you're writing for a college class, it's still formal writing, but the situation is a little different. Your readers are professors who have been paid — precious little — to read your essay, so that's what they will do whether your opening does its job or not.

However, your essay will be more successful if you write it professionally and make sure that the opening tells your professor what to expect. When you do that, you make their job easier. That's nice for them. An effective opening also makes it easier for them to see where your essay sticks to that task and where it strays, and that helps them talk to you about what works and what doesn't work in your essay. That's nice for you.

The Ingredients for a Good Opening

The opening for a college essay is usually brief — just one or two paragraphs — even for a longer paper. That's because it doesn't take too much time to tell readers what to expect from the essay. Here is a two-paragraph opening for an essay about Jane Eyre, the title character in Charlotte Brontë's novel:

> Mistakes are an unavoidable and necessary part of life. It is human nature to make mistakes, and it is through mistakes that we learn to be better humans. However, our worst mistakes are the ones we keep repeating without learning from the consequences. We see this in the title character of Charlotte Brontë's novel, *Jane Eyre*. Jane makes many mistakes along her pathway from childhood to adulthood in the first half of this novel. In some cases, she learns from her mistakes and improves herself. In most cases, she does not. What is Jane's worst mistake? Her worst mistake is that

she often follows her heart without thinking about the consequences. This is her worst mistake because no matter how much she harms or endangers herself by doing this, she keeps repeating the same mistake over and over, with worse and worse consequences.

A mistake is "an error in action, calculation, opinion, or judgment caused by poor reasoning, carelessness, insufficient knowledge, etc." ("mistake," def. 1). Jane's worst mistake is an error in judgment, and it is caused by poor reasoning. In fact, it is caused by a total lack of reasoning. Instead of taking the time to think about the actual consequences of past actions or the potential consequences of future actions, she blindly follows her heart. In this first half of the novel, that never works out very well for Jane. Time after time, she puts herself and others at risk by letting her feelings guide her. Jane makes this mistake so often that it would take a paper as long as the novel to cover all the examples. However, we can see this mistake clearly from a few key examples in the first chapters of the novel, so that is what this paper will primarily examine.

This introduction tells you exactly what to expect from this paper. It stretches over two paragraphs because it introduces more than the minimum required ingredients. Speaking of which, there are three minimum required ingredients:

1. **Topic:** The topic of this paper will be the mistakes made by the title character of Charlotte Brontë's novel, *Jane Eyre*. This is introduced in the fourth sentence of the first paragraph, and it is reinforced by references in both paragraphs.

2. **Focus:** You can't cover everything related to any topic, so the opening also needs to tell readers what you will do with that topic. Maybe you will judge it. Maybe you will interpret what it means. Maybe you will propose a solution for it — if it's a problem. In this case, the focus is to judge which is the biggest mistake Jane makes in the first half of this novel. That is introduced by a question in the first paragraph — "What is Jane's worst mistake?" It's reinforced by the repetition of "worst mistake" in two other sentences, one in the first paragraph and one in the second.

3. **Thesis:** The main idea is stated immediately after the question that introduces the focus of the essay — "Her worst mistake is that she often follows her heart without thinking about the consequences." The next sentence in the first paragraph reinforces this by explaining why this is her worst mistake. This will be the main idea that the paper explains.

The three required ingredients are all present in the first paragraph. That's good because they are the most important things to introduce. You need to get to the most important stuff first. However, the opening can do more than just introduce these three key ingredients.

An opening can optionally define an important term that will be used throughout. General terms like "valuable" or "effective" or "wrong" can be understood in so many different ways that it's a good idea to tell your readers *exactly* what you mean. This paper takes a few sentences to define "mistake" at the start of paragraph two. It identifies both the type of mistake — "error of judgment" — and the cause — "poor reasoning." I'm not sure that this is really necessary for this opening because the nature of the mistake will become clear in the body of the essay, but it doesn't hurt.

An opening can also tell readers what sort of the evidence to expect from the essay. In this case, the introduction of the evidence comes at the end of the second paragraph. The student writer whines a little that she would have to write an enormous paper to cover all of Jane's mistakes, so she is taking the easy way out by only looking at a few representative examples from the first chapter. This does a couple of things for the student writer. First, it tells the readers what to expect more precisely — expect to look mostly at the early chapters. The second thing it does is to defend the writer from a skeptical reader — say the professor who assigned this paper — who might otherwise complain that paper hasn't considered all the relevant evidence. It tells the reader, "I am so sorry, but if I had to look at all the relevant evidence, this paper would be way too long — even for someone like you who loves to read student papers until late in the evening. So for your sake as well as mine, I am forced to narrow my focus just a little."

The Formal Reader Does Not Require Hooking

At some point in your long journey through English classes, you were probably told that one job for the introduction is to "hook the reader," to dangle some juicy bait in front your fish-like readers and hope that they will be dumb enough to bite. With formal writing, there's some truth to this advice — but not much.

> "Formal readers don't need to be hooked. If your paper has what they are looking for, they will hook themselves."

The little bit of truth is that it doesn't hurt to make a formal paper a little more inviting with some reader bait. I'll talk more about that in a minute. However, that only works when your opening clearly tells the reader what to expect — as in the three required ingredients of topic, focus, and thesis. Most good formal openings make no effort at all to hook the readers because formal readers don't need to be hooked. If your paper has what they are looking for, they will hook themselves.

This hooking of readers belongs to informal writing, which is what you have been doing until recently. With informal writing — from magazines to blogs to websites — the reading is optional. To get readers to read, you have to make them curious to read more. Think about those tabloid stories you see while standing in line at the grocery store — a movie star gives birth to a bat, the Queen of England secretly dates Mel Gibson, the distinguished senator from Florida wrestles alligators on the Senate floor. Those tabloids are competing against candy bars for your attention. They know how much you like candy bars, too, so they stop at nothing to hook you.

With formal writing, you have to be careful about trying too hard to hook your readers. Even the no-nonsense readers of professional writing can't help themselves from getting hooked *a little* by some cleverness in the opening. A little humor, a relevant cultural reference, or a short anecdote can still bring quiet pleasure to a professional reader — if the essay is also relevant to their interests. These readers are people, too, mostly, so they like to be amused as much as the next person. You just have to be careful to not work too hard at that. If these readers notice that you're trying to hook them, they will be annoyed rather than hooked.

Consider the minor "hook" at the beginning of this *Jane Eyre* essay. Before introducing the actual topic of the essay, the writer takes three sentences to build a little bridge with the readers:

> Mistakes are an unavoidable and necessary part of life. It is human nature to make mistakes, and it is through mistakes that we learn to be better humans. However, our worst mistakes are the ones we keep repeating without learning from the consequences.

That hook isn't a *bad* thing to do. It might remind the readers of their worst mistakes, and that might stir up some emotions that make the paper more engaging. But it's hardly necessary. This writer could launch right into the introduction of the topic without trying to hook anyone. The opening would be just as effective.

Especially while you are still learning the basics of how to write college essays, your openings should probably stick to the main ingredients of the opening — topic, focus, and thesis. Consider how the *Jane Eyre* opening would look if it stuck to the basics. It would only be one paragraph long, and that paragraph would look something like this:

> In the first half of Charlotte Brontë's novel, *Jane Eyre*, the title character makes many mistakes along her pathway from childhood to adulthood in the first half of this novel. What is Jane's worst mistake? Her worst mistake is that she often follows her heart without thinking about the consequences. This is her worst mistake because no matter how much she harms or endangers herself by doing this, she never learns from the mistake but keeps repeating the same mistake over and over, with worse and worse consequences.

This works, too, because all three required ingredients are present. Our expectations are still a little fuzzy, of course. We're not sure what standard is being used to judge her mistakes. We're not sure what sort of evidence will be used. We'll have to figure that out as we move into the body of the essay. But that's okay, and it's especially okay when you are just getting started with college essays.

Body Paragraphs

While opening paragraphs have a lot of different things to do all at once, the body paragraphs focus on just one task. They are the worker bees of the essay. Each body paragraph might explain one reason, define one key term, offer one example, or present one small set of information. It does that one job, and when the job is done — because it is a good worker bee — it stops.

Worker bees may only have one job to do, but they still live rich and meaningful lives. It's the same with body paragraphs. They have rich and meaningful sentences, and those sentences work together in complex and interesting ways. Body paragraphs also connect with other body paragraphs to form larger ideas. We'll take a look at how this works with body paragraphs from the same essay about Jane Eyre.

Topic Sentences and Supporting Sentences

To talk about body paragraphs, we need two new technical terms — **topic sentence** and **supporting sentences**. You understand now that a topic is the subject that you are writing about. You might think then that a topic sentence has something to do with the topic of your essay. That's a reasonable conclusion, student writer, but I'm afraid you couldn't be more wrong. A topic sentence is a single sentence that tells your readers what a paragraph will explain. It's like a thesis statement for the paragraph.

The rest of the sentences in the paragraph are supporting sentences. What they support is the topic sentence, and they do that by explaining in more detail whatever the topic sentence promises. If the topic sentence promises to give readers an example of the thesis, then the supporting sentences explain that example in detail. If the topic sentence tells readers that there are three main objections to the thesis, then the supporting sentences patiently provide detailed explanations all three objections.

Consider this paragraph from the body of the *Jane Eyre* essay:

> **One early example of this error in judgment comes from chapter 1 when Jane has a fight with her cousin, John Reed.** Although she is young, she has lived in this household long enough to know (if she were to think

about it) that her cousin is just a loud and harmless bully, and that the best way to deal with bullies is to not let them get under your skin. Jane, however, doesn't think this through, and that leads to her error in judgment. She lashes out at her cousin, calling him a "wicked and cruel boy" and adding, "You are like a murderer — you are like a slave-driver — You are like the Roman emperors!" (13). It might have felt good for Jane to say this after John had hit her in the head with a book (12), but it was still a mistake, and it brought serious consequences. Mrs. Reed orders Jane locked in the red-room (14), and this becomes more than just a "time out" for naughty behavior. The experience terrorizes Jane, and in response to that upheaval, Mrs. Reed segregates Jane from the rest of the family. Jane is forced to sleep in a small closet, and she must eat alone (29).

The topic sentence (in **bold**) tells us that this paragraph will present one example of Jane's mistake, a fight in chapter 1. The rest of the sentences are supporting sentences that explain the mistake in detail. First, the supporting sentences tell us that Jane should have known better than to fight with her cousin. Second, they provide a detailed, blow-by-blow account of how she acts without thinking. Finally, to prove that this was a mistake they summarize the unfortunate consequences. All those details make this an effective little worker bee paragraph.

Another way to think about the topic sentence and supporting sentences is that the topic sentence creates a box for the supporting sentences. All supporting sentences then have to belong in that box. If a cereal box says "Fruit Loops," then that box better be full of Fruit Loops and only Fruit Loops. If I open it and find Raisin Bran, I will be confused and sad. In the same way, if a topic sentence promises one of Jane Eyre's mistakes, then the supporting sentences better talk about one of Jane Eyre's mistakes or your readers will be confused and sad.

In the example above, the topic sentence tells us to expect one example of Jane's general mistake. That's the box. All of the supporting sentences help to explain this example, so they belong in that box. You don't have any sentences talking about what a jerk John Reed is. You don't have anything about the weather that afternoon. You're only given what you are told to expect, information that is relevant to this particular example, information that belongs to this box.

Use Two Body Paragraphs to Present One Larger Idea

Sometimes a supporting idea will be too complex to explain in just one paragraph. Formal writing allows for much longer paragraphs, but even professionals don't want to see a paragraph stretch on for page after page. That looks boring — even to them. The solution is to divide the large supporting idea into two or more logical parts and make each its own paragraph, with its own topic sentence and supporting sentences. You then link the related paragraphs together with transitional phrases or sentences that show readers that you're still talking about the same general idea.

Here's an example of this from the second and third body paragraphs of the same student essay, and again, the topic sentences are in **bold** for your visual enjoyment:

> **In spite of these fairly severe consequences, Jane makes the same mistake soon after her red-room experience by physically attacking her cousin.** Jane sees her cousin John mocking her, and because she hasn't learned anything from the consequences of her last mistake, she punches him in the nose (29). Her mistake doesn't stop there. When John complains to Mrs. Reed, Mrs. Reed says, "Don't talk to me about her, John: I told you not to go near her; she is not worthy of notice; I do not choose that either you or your sisters should associate with her" (29). Then, "without at all deliberating on [her] words," Jane verbally attacks Mrs. Reed by crying out, "They are not fit to associate with me" (30). It doesn't stop there, either. When Mrs. Reed grabs Jane and hurls her into the nursery, Jane hits back, again without thinking:
>
> > "What would Uncle Reed say to you, if he were alive?" was my scarcely voluntary demand. I say scarcely voluntary, for it seemed as if my tongue pronounced words without my will consenting to their utterance: something spoke out of me over which I had no control. (30)
>
> That "something" is her emotions, and they keep sending words out of her mouth, too. When this question staggers Mrs. Reed, Jane follows up with a second blow to Mrs. Reed's gut: "My Uncle Reed is in heaven, and can see all you do and think; and so can papa and mama: they know how you shut me up all day long, and how you wish me dead" (30). Mrs. Reed eventually regains her composure and boxes Jane's ears (31), but the damage has been done.

> **This time, the consequences for Jane's mistake are more severe than a trip to the red-room or dinner by herself.** Mrs. Reed's next move is to remove Jane from Gateshead entirely by sending her to Lowood school for poor and neglected girls. She arranges for a visit from the "harsh and prim" Mr. Brocklehurst, the headmaster at Lowood Institution (34). After a brief interview that consists mostly of talking about how deceitful Jane is (34-35), Mr. Brocklehurst leaves and Jane is on her way to Lowood. Jane might think she wants to go to school (27), but as she will find in later chapters, Lowood is a miserable and dangerous place. The girls there live on bread and water. The building is barely heated. Jane will suffer at Lowood, and if she hadn't been the main character in this novel, she could easily have died like her friend Helen Burns (85) or dozens of other Lowood girls who will later die from typhus (79).

This two-paragraph explanation of Jane's second mistake follows the same pattern as the earlier one-paragraph example. First, it states how Jane should have known better by then. Next, it explains in detail how Jane acts without thinking about the consequences. Then it examines the consequences. The explanation is divided into two paragraphs at a logical place — between the actions and the consequences. The first paragraph provides details about this more complex mistake. The second paragraph then provides details about the nature of the consequences.

This writer helps you to see that these paragraphs are two parts of one supporting idea in a couple ways. First, look at the topic sentences. The first one introduces a new example. We know, then, that this is the start of a new supporting point for the thesis. The second topic sentence, however, refers back to that same example by saying "this time" instead of introducing whatever comes next. The last sentence of the first paragraph also helps tie the two paragraphs together. When it says that "the damage has been done," it hints at the consequences of Jane's action, which will be explained in the next paragraph. These brief references do a nice job of linking the two paragraphs together. The reader only needs a little help to see how two worker-bee paragraphs work together to form a worker-bee partnership.

By the way, it looks like there are four paragraphs here because of that block quotation from *Jane Eyre*. Block quotations like this are considered part of the paragraph that introduces them, so it's not really a separate paragraph. You'll notice, too, that after that quoted paragraph ends, the first line of the next paragraph is not indented. Indenting the first line shows readers that a new paragraph is starting. When you don't indent, it tells the reader that this is part of original paragraph and not the start of a new one.

Organize Sentences within a Body Paragraph

Everything makes more sense when it's organized. Compare these two paragraphs:

> The consequences for Jane's mistake this time are more severe than a trip to the red-room or segregation from the other children. Mrs. Reed's next move is to remove Jane from Gateshead entirely by sending her to Lowood school for poor and neglected girls. Jane might think she wants to go to school (27), but as she will find in later chapters, Lowood is a miserable and dangerous place. The girls there live on bread and water. The building is barely heated. Jane will suffer at Lowood, and if she hadn't been the main character in this novel, she could easily have died like her friend Helen Burns (85) or dozens of other Lowood girls who die from typhus (79).

> The consequences for Jane's mistake this time are more severe than a trip to the red-room or segregation from the other children. Jane will suffer at Lowood, and if she hadn't been the main character in this novel, she could easily have died like her friend Helen Burns (85) or dozens of other Lowood girls who die from typhus (79). Jane might think she wants to go to school (27), but as she will find in later chapters, Lowood is a miserable and dangerous place. The building is barely heated. Mrs. Reed's next move is to remove Jane from Gateshead entirely by sending her to Lowood school for poor and neglected girls. The girls there live on bread and water.

The only difference between these two paragraphs is the organization of the supporting sentences. In the first paragraph, the order of supporting sentences follows a **chronological** pattern of organization. In the second paragraph, there's no pattern. The sentences all fit into the cereal box of the topic sentence, but they're presented randomly. You can still figure out the topic sentence idea, but the lack of organization means you have to work harder.

In the *Jane Eyre* paragraphs you've seen so far, the supporting sentences follow a chronological pattern. In the paragraph about Jane's first mistake, it's a pattern of what Jane does and what happens afterwards. In the two paragraphs about Jane's second mistake, the first paragraph looks at what Jane does, step by step, and the second paragraph looks at the immediate consequences and how they will get worse in later years. Because these supporting sentences describe something Jane does, it makes sense to organize them chronologically in the order in which it happens.

Below you'll see another two-paragraph mistake of Jane's to round out the body of this student essay. As you read it, try to figure out how the supporting sentences are organized. And, for added pleasure, look for any words or phrases that point out what sort of pattern is being used to put the sentences in this order. Here you go:

> **Before Jane leaves Gateshead, she makes the same mistake one last time by attacking her aunt directly.** Following Jane's interview with Lowood School's dean, Mr. Brocklehurst, Jane cannot get over the sting of her aunt calling her a liar during the interview (38). It will be no surprise by now that she "felt every word as acutely" and "a passion of resentment fomented" within her (38). When Mrs. Reed notices Jane fomenting, she tells Jane to take it to her room (39). If Jane were to think about how badly things go for her when she follows her emotions, she would have taken it to her room and fomented in private. However, that's not how Jane operates. Instead, she makes the same stupid mistake:
>
>> Speak I must: I had been trodden on severely, and must turn: but how? What strength had I to dart retaliation at my antagonist? I gathered my energies and launched them in this blunt sentence: —
>> "I am not deceitful: if I were, I should say I loved you; but I declare I do not love you: I dislike you the worst of anybody in the world except John Reed...." (39)
>
> The conversation goes downhill from there. Even after Mrs. Reed uncharacteristically tries to make amends with Jane (40), Jane will have none of it. "You told Mr. Brocklehurst I had a bad character, a deceitful disposition," she says, "and I'll let everybody at Lowood know what you are, and what you have done" (40).
>
> **The immediate and long-term consequences for Jane's third mistake are the most severe.** Mrs. Reed promises to send Jane to Lowood quickly, a promise that she keeps. In fact, she sends Jane to Lowood for

keeps, forcing Jane to stay at Lowood all year round without any contact with or support from Mrs. Reed or Gateshead. Jane essentially becomes an orphan for a second time, and she spends the next several years living in poverty, abuse, and disease. Jane permanently earns Mrs. Reed's hatred with this passionate little speech of hers, and that leads to more serious, long-term consequences. While Jane is still at Lowood, Jane's surviving uncle writes Mrs. Reed because he has become rich and wants to take care of Jane (241). Because she now hates Jane so much, Mrs. Reed writes back saying that Jane is dead (242). Jane therefore misses out on those riches when they could have done her some good. She continues to suffer away at Lowood. Later, because she has no money from her uncle, she is forced to hire herself out as a governess at Thornfield. In the months that follow, she suffers a wide range of terrible consequences. All of those consequences are great for the twists and turns of a gothic novel, but they are terrible consequences for an actual person. Jane could have avoided them all if she had learned from the consequences of this mistake instead of repeating it.

So what patterns do you see within the supporting sentences of these two paragraphs? If you say "chronological," you're right, even if that was just a lucky guess. That's one pattern of organization here. However, that's not the only pattern. Our student writer also uses textual and ranking patterns.

A **textual** pattern uses the location of information within the text — a published work of some sort — to organize that information. As you look at the paragraphs above, you can see that they just kind of march through the book's pages, from 38 to 39 to 40 and then a big jump down to 241 and 242. This overlaps with the chronological pattern because the novel is also organized chronologically.

Another pattern that this student writer uses is **ranking**. Ranking organizes the parts of something from least to most or most to least — least to most points scored, most to least important, least to most expensive, and so on. You can rank things according to whatever quality makes the most sense for your idea. In the second paragraph above, the writer also ranks two sets of consequences by the quality of seriousness. The first consequence is that Jane is sent away from home "for keeps." That's serious. Then come "more serious" consequences.

Organize Paragraphs within the Body

Organization happens at two levels in the body of the essay — with the supporting sentences within each paragraph and with the paragraphs within the body. You can see above how organizing the sentences within a paragraph makes it easier for readers to understand the topic sentence idea. The same thing happens with the paragraphs within the body of an essay. If those paragraphs are arranged according to a pattern, your readers are more likely to see how the body as a whole works together to explain your thesis.

In this student's essay, one pattern is chronological:

1. **At the start:** Jane says mean things to her cousin John.

2. **Days later:** Jane punches John and says mean things about all the Reed children.

3. **Months later:** Jane says mean things to Mrs. Reed.

This is a natural pattern to use because the topic is a person in a story, and both people and stories happen chronologically. No lives are lived out of order.

Another pattern that the writer uses is a textual pattern:

1. **Page 13:** Jane says mean things to her cousin John.

2. **Pages 29-30:** Jane punches John and says mean things about all the Reed children.

3. **Pages 38-39:** Jane says mean things to Mrs. Reed.

Textual patterns are useful whenever the topic is something that is written. They use the structure of the topic itself to organize the evidence. A third pattern that this student writer uses is **ranking**. In this essay, it makes sense to consider the seriousness of the consequences for Jane's bad decisions, and that's what the writer does:

1. **Serious:** Jane is segregated from the other children within the Gateshead house.

2. **More serious:** Jane is sent away from the relative comfort of Gates-head to the poverty and dangers of Lowood.

3. **Most serious:** Jane is kept apart from her rich uncle and the advantages he wants to give her.

Just about any pattern will work as long as the readers can see what that pattern is. For this student writer, the three patterns I've mentioned all make sense for this thesis and this evidence. However, the student writer could have organized the same evidence in a more superficial way — by a location pattern, for example:

1. **In the library:** Jane says mean things to her cousin John.

2. **In the hallway**: Jane punches John and says mean things about all the Reed children.

3. **In the parlor:** Jane says mean things to Mrs. Reed.

The location of these events isn't related to the thesis, so it's not as useful as the chronological or ranking patterns, but it still works when it comes to helping readers make sense of the whole. Any pattern will do as long as the essay sticks to that pattern.

Transitions and Topic Sentences Point Out Organization

The organization patterns are hinted at by **transitions** in these paragraphs. Transitional words or phrases connect sentences to other sentences or paragraphs to other paragraphs. Sometimes transitions act like a bridge that connects two ideas directly, as you can see from the third example of Jane's general mistake:

> If Jane were to think about how badly things go for her when she follows her emotions, she would have taken it to her room and fomented in private. **However**, that's not how Jane operates.

Sometimes transitional words or phrases show how a sentence fits into a larger pattern — in this case, a chronological pattern:

Following Jane's interview with Lowood School's dean

When Mrs. Reed notices Jane fomenting

The conversation goes downhill **from there**.

Even **after** Mrs. Reed uncharacteristically tries to make amends

In this same example, you can also see that this chronological pattern is overlapped by textual pattern — page 38, then 39, and then 40.

On pages 41 and 42 of this humble book, the second paragraph of the student example looks at the consequences of Jane's third unreflective outburst. In the topic sentence, the word "consequences" is a transition that shows how this paragraph is related to the one before. Her mistake happens first, and the consequences happen afterwards. The topic sentence also introduces a chronological pattern within the paragraph by saying that the consequences are "immediate" (first) and "long-term" (later). The first set of sentences summarizes the immediate consequences. The second set summarizes the long-term consequences.

Halfway through the paragraph, the student writer adds this phrase about the long-term consequence: "more serious, long-term consequences." That phrase tells us that there is also a ranking pattern:

1. **Serious:** immediate consequences

2. **More serious:** long-term consequences

Let's see how transitions works now with the final paragraph of the body of this essay:

> In all three examples above, Jane never learns to control her emotions and think about what she is doing. **The same basic mistake continues throughout the entire first half of the novel.** While she is at Lowood, for example, she climbs into bed with the dying Helen Burns even though everyone wisely tells her not to because Helen is dying of consumption, a contagious disease (85). Later, when she is living at Thornfield, she lets her emotions for Rochester cloud her judgment repeatedly. She doesn't tell anyone about the fire or "Grace Poole" because she is already infatuated with Rochester (151-53). She then agrees to keep the attack on Mason secret

because Rochester gives her, not a reason of any kind, but a rose (218). Still later, even after Mrs. Fairfax clearly hints that Jane needs to watch her step as Rochester's fiancée, (266-67), she remains set on marrying Rochester. It would take a paper as long as this novel to cover all the times Jane makes this mistake because from start to finish, she refuses think things through when her heart is aroused by any kind of strong feeling.

Instead of presenting one specific idea in detail, this paragraph is summarizing a lot of information. If the entire essay were made of summarizing paragraphs like this, it wouldn't be very effective because readers want detailed information to see what you mean and why you mean it. When you have a body full of summarizing paragraphs, it means you need to narrow your focus to a smaller part of the topic so that you could get into more detail and cover it more completely. However, as you saw, this writer *did* get into details when looking at Jane's early behavior, so the body is still effective.

But we're here to talk about transitions. The first transition comes in the first sentence. When the writer says, "In all three examples above," she connects this paragraph to the preceding body paragraphs. In formal writing, "above" means "before." Page 1 is "above" page 3. The second sentence — the topic sentence — connects the early pattern to the first half of the novel:

> The same basic mistake continues throughout the entire first half of the novel.

These transitions aren't telling us about organization. They are telling us about how the ideas in the body of the essay are connected to each other. In this case, the transitions tell us that examples from the body paragraphs "above" are related logically to the examples in this paragraph because it is the same mistake.

Other transitions tell us how the supporting sentences in this paragraph are organized:

> **While** she is at Lowood

> **Later, when** she is living at Thornfield

> She **then** agrees

> **Still later,** even **after** Mrs. Fairfax clearly hints that

How are these sentences organized? If you said "chronologically," you are getting the hang of this. Good for you, student writer. If you also said "textually," then I couldn't be more pleased with your progress. As you saw from the page numbers, the chronologically arranged sentences are also coming to us in the order in which they appear in the text.

Closing Paragraphs

The closing paragraphs of a college essay have two jobs to do. First, they must remind readers about the ideas and information from the body of the essay. Second, they must explain to readers one last time how the ideas and information from the body illustrate and defend the essay's main idea.

With shorter essays like the *Jane Eyre* essay — and yes, believe it or not, this is fairly short college essay — you can accomplish both jobs in one paragraph because there isn't as much to summarize from the body. With longer essays that are more detailed and complex, you should take much more time in closing so that you're able to summarize all the key points and present your main idea in all its complexity. With scientific papers, your closing might be a third the length of the essay.

Here is the closing paragraph from this student's *Jane Eyre* essay:

> Some might look at Jane's many errors of judgment and say, "Bravo, Jane! Follow your heart!" It's satisfying to cheer for the underdog who stands up to oppressors, to cheer for David as he takes on Goliath. Because Jane is clearly the underdog in this first half of the novel, we can enjoy cheering for her as she stands up to her Goliaths in the form of her cousins, her aunt, the oppressive conditions at Lowood, and so on. However, while David in the Bible story is guided by noble inner convictions when he stands up to his Goliath, Jane is guided only by blind emotions. That's a mistake, and because Jane keeps making the same mistake in spite of all the misery it brings into her life, it is her worst mistake in the first half of this novel. We should not cheer for the way this underdog stands up to her oppressors. We should instead pity her.

The first thing to notice about this closing paragraph is that it is a fully explained paragraph. It's not one or two sentences long. I point this out because so many student writers will end an otherwise good essay with something hideous like this:

> In conclusion, Jane's biggest mistake was that she acted without thinking, as the body of the essay has shown.

Foolish student writers!

Your closing paragraphs must be detailed and complete — just like those detailed and complete paragraphs in the body of the essay. For those of you who know baseball, the body of your essay needs to hit a home run, and the closing needs to run slowly around the bases, waving to the crowd, making it official. Don't stop before you're actually finished just because the essay feels finished. You're done when you're done.

The closing from the *Jane Eyre* essay sets a good example for how to remind readers about the body of the essay and then connect that information to the thesis. It does the first job with two different references — "Jane's many errors of judgment" and "she stands up to her Goliaths in the form of her cousins, her aunt, the oppressive conditions at Lowood, and so on." That's not overly detailed. The writer could be more specific about the examples that were present in the body, but these two brief references are still enough to remind us about the evidence and ideas in the body of the essay. The closing then restates the main idea of the essay:

> However, while David in the Bible story is guided by noble inner convictions when he stands up to his Goliath, Jane is guided only by blind emotions. That's a mistake, and because Jane keeps making the same mistake in spite of all the misery it brings into her life, it is her worst mistake in the first half of this novel.

It reminds us what Jane's mistake is, and it explains why this is her worst mistake in the first half of the novel. The phrasing here is close to the phrasing of the thesis statement in opening paragraph, and that's good, too. It echoes the opening, helping readers to look backward at the essay and see that we have closure here, that the essay has kept its promise by explaining this idea.

The closing also offers something extra, and that makes it more than just okay. Besides fulfilling those two required duties, it adds the idea about cheering for underdogs and shows why that isn't appropriate in Jane's case. A lot of readers do like to cheer for Jane, and many would say that she is guided by noble principles. This writer, however, has made the case in the body of the essay that Jane is guided by blind emotions. Now the writer concludes by showing how this main idea can inform our own natural urge to cheer for Jane as an underdog. This is an interesting twist, so it gives us a new way of thinking about the usefulness of the paper's main idea.

Writing One Paragraph at a Time

For many new college writers, a paper like this *Jane Eyre* essay — with its mass of well-developed paragraphs — seems a little out of reach. And it might actually be out of reach, too — at least at first.

Formal writing takes practice. As a formal *reader*, you have to unravel what those long paragraphs have to say, one sentence at a time. As a formal *writer*, you also have to be patient. You have to explain yourself in plenty of detail, which translates into plenty of supporting sentences. It won't take you very long to get the hang of this, but you do have to make the effort, and it won't be particularly easy at first.

Your work with formal writing will be easier to bear if you break your task down into paragraphs. As a reader, that means figuring out the idea for each paragraph before moving on to the next one. As a writer, that means taking the time to write one good paragraph at a time. Start with a precise topic sentence. Then make sure that every supporting sentence stays within the box of that topic sentence, that each one provides detailed information that makes your topic sentence idea easier to understand. Organizing those supporting sentences — either before or after you write them — will also help the paragraph to be more effective.

Once you get the hang of formal writing, you'll see that the pleasure it offers — that's right, *pleasure* — far outweighs the superficial pleasures of a fun, quick, informal paper. Thinking takes longer than not thinking, but it rewards you with all sorts of discoveries and insights that you will enjoy having in your brain — and sharing with others. With even a little practice, you will begin to see the advantages and the pleasures of taking your time and presenting your thinking in detail.

The key is just to slow down. When you're reading, understand one paragraph before you move on to the next. When you're writing, make sure you have fully explained the topic sentence of paragraph before you start writing the next paragraph.

The Big Ideas

This chapter introduced you to the three types of paragraphs in a college essay — opening, body, and closing paragraphs. It also talked about how these formal paragraphs operate. Here are the big ideas:

1. Informal and formal paragraphs: Informal paragraphs are visual. They break up the essays so that the essay looks more readable. Formal paragraphs are idea-based. A paragraph ends when it has done its job of introducing or explaining one supporting idea.

2. Opening paragraphs: The opening paragraphs tell readers what to expect from the essay that follows. At a minimum, it tells readers about the **topic**, **focus**, and **thesis** of an essay. In formal writing, openings do not have to hook the reader, but it's okay to entice the reader a little.

3. Body paragraphs: Body paragraphs explain one idea or present one set of information. A topic sentence tells readers what the paragraph will do — like a thesis statement for that paragraph. Supporting sentences explain the topic sentence with more detailed information.

4. Closing paragraphs: Closing paragraphs must summarize the information from the body of the essay and then remind readers how that information helps to explain and defend the main idea. These should be full, detailed paragraphs. Don't wimp out.

Chapter 3
Paragraphs Are Made of Grammatical Sentences

In chapter 2, we looked at the difference between informal paragraphs and formal paragraphs — a difference of looks versus meaning. With informal writing, you use paragraphs to make the page look more inviting to readers. With formal writing, each paragraph must present its own idea.

There's a similar difference between informal and formal sentences, but with sentences, it's a difference of sound versus meaning. With informal writing, you use sentences to capture the sound of your voice. With formal writing, you use sentences to capture your ideas. Each sentence must state one idea — an opinion, a summary, a piece of information — that makes sense on its own, without any help from other sentences. Your sentences must be **grammatical sentences**, in other words, sentences that follow the rules of English grammar.

Among writing professors, there's some disagreement about how — or whether — to teach students the rules of grammar. Some colleagues tell me that students just need to read more, that the rules of grammar will sink in on their own. These colleagues were raised in the 1970s, a decade defined by bell-bottom pants and optimistic educational theories. Others tell me I'm a fool to even try teaching the rules of grammar, that you're just going to use grammar checkers, that the technical terms will put you to sleep, that the English language is dying because of smartphones, that all is lost, the sky is falling, and so on.

They're probably right.

However, every class I teach is full of otherwise confident students who are painfully anxious about their writing. Why so anxious? Because they don't know what they're doing. They lack technical skills. Whenever they must write grammatical sentences, they have to guess about every single sentence — or trust a grammar checker, which is another way of guessing — and guessing is stressful, especially when you know that your guesses are going to be judged by critical readers.

So although it's probably something you will figure out on your own or a complete waste of time, I believe it is a fundamental human right for you to at least be introduced to the rules of English grammar and formal punctuation.

That's what we'll do in this and the next chapter.

Informal Sentences

Informal sentences usually make sense as part of a conversation. Sometimes they make sense because they follow the rules of English grammar. Sometimes they make sense because of how they fit into a longer conversation or paragraph. Here are three perfectly good informal sentences that work together to tell one of the best jokes I know:

> So this skeleton walks into a bar.
> Says to the bartender, give me a beer.
> And a mop.

Get it? Each sentence makes sense when you're telling this joke to your friends because the sentences work together as a complete unit. But if — after you stop laughing — you take the middle sentence out and say it on its own, it doesn't make as much sense:

> Says to the bartender, give me a beer.

Who says this to the bartender? Your friends have no idea. It's no longer a complete thought. The last sentence is even worse on its own:

> And a mop.

If you were to walk up to your friends and say "And a mop," they'd slowly back away from you because that doesn't make any sense at all — plus you've been acting a little weird lately. Moody. But again, it's fine when it's part of a longer conversation. In fact, it's more than fine. It's a great punch line for a terrific joke.

You learned to make informal sentences by listening to and imitating the high-pitched voices of the adults who were drawn to the baby version of you like so many hummingbirds to a flower. For most of the writing that you will do in this life, you can get by with writing how you speak. That's what you do with text messages, e-mail, online posts, meaningful poems about sunsets and kittens, or sticky notes on the back door asking your beloved to take out the recycling — it's his week for recycling, after all, but the recycling just keeps piling up under the sink like a tiny disaster area. For these types of informal writing, grammatical sentences are entirely optional.

In fact, the only real problem with informal sentences is just that they aren't good enough for formal writing. They don't capture your ideas precisely enough, and when your writing is judged by formal readers of any sort, they make you look less intelligent than you are. To be effective as a writer of academic and other formal papers, your sentences must be grammatical.

Grammatical Sentences

A grammatical sentence is a group of words that makes sense on its own because it follows the rules of grammar. Grammar rules define all the different ways that words can be combined to create sentences. By following the rules of grammar, your sentence captures one of your ideas — but on its own, without having to rely on the context of the paragraph to make sense.

The main rules are fairly simple. They start with the two required ingredients for any sentence — a noun and a verb. But the rules become increasingly complex in order to explain how complicated sentences are able to capture complicated ideas. Those rules are defined using technical terms, and those technical terms are defined by other technical terms — which are defined by still more technical terms. In other words, the rules of grammar are like anything else. If you're going to learn it, you have to dive in and really learn it. You can't just *kind of* learn it.

Learning the rules of grammar will require the use of technical terms. If these technical terms put you to sleep at times, so be it. Enjoy your readily interpreted dreams, and then come back and study the technical terms a little more. They will make more sense when you're rested. Once you begin to see how they apply to your own sentences, you're 90 percent there with grammar. And seriously, if you can learn technical terms like "phylum" or "schema" or "sine wave" — and you can — then you can put on your big-boy or big-girl pants and learn to use these grammatical terms, too.

We'll start with the basics.

The Clause

The first technical term to learn is **clause**. A clause is a group of words that captures an idea. It captures an idea because it contains two vital ingredients — a noun and then a verb that tells us something about that noun.

If the clause makes sense entirely on its own, it's called an **independent clause** — also known as a grammatical sentence. If, for one reason or another, the clause doesn't make sense entirely on its own, it's called a **dependent clause**. These dependent clauses are dependent because they have to be a sub-unit within an independent clause to make sense.

The Independent Clause

Here are some independent clauses from the first half of another terrific joke. The noun is in **bold** and the verb is underlined:

> **A duck** walks boldly into a bar to order a beer.
> **She** orders a Pilsner.

> **The old bartender with the Grateful Dead tattoo** is confused.

Right away, you can see that I lied about clauses. These independent clauses do not consist of just *one* noun and *one* verb. In fact, the only one-noun and one-verb sentence you'll probably ever use is "**I** do." Other than that powerful little gem, your sentences will be longer and more complex.

So instead of "noun" and "verb," we need to use the terms "noun phrase" and "verb phrase." A **noun phrase** consists of either a pronoun (such as "she") or one noun (such as "bartender") and any words or phrases that help to describe that noun (such "the," "old," and "with the Grateful Dead tattoo"). A **verb phrase** consists of one verb (such as "walks") and any words or phrases that help to explain that verb (such as "boldly," "into a bar," and "to order a beer"). To be more accurate, then, the first rule of grammar is that an independent clause — a grammatical sentence — consists of a noun phrase and a verb phrase.

However, that's not quite true, either.

You see, even within the main noun phrase and verb phrase of these little sentences, there are other noun phrases and verb phrases helping to explain the main noun and main verb. One noun phrase, "a Pilsner," helps to explain the verb "orders" by telling us what the duck orders. And there's a verb-like phrase, "to order a beer," that helps to explain the verb "walks" by telling us why the duck walks into the bar. The noun phrase "a Grateful Dead tattoo" is also part of the explanation about which bartender was on duty during this joke.

To define how the sentence works, then, we need to use two more technical terms — subject and predicate. The **subject** is the *main* noun phrase for an independent clause. It's the main thing that the verb tells us about. In the sentences of the joke, that's what's in bold. The **predicate** is the *main* verb phrase in a clause. It either tells us what the subject does, or it describes the subject. In those same sentences, that's what's underlined.

To be more precise, then, a clause is a group of words that capture an idea because they have a subject and a predicate. If the clause makes sense entirely on its own, it's called an independent clause. If the clause doesn't make sense entirely on its own, it's called a dependent clause.

The Dependent Clause

A dependent clause still has a noun phrase and a verb phrase, so it still contains an idea. However, something has happened that makes it a supporting idea instead of a main idea. For example, the subject might have turned into a relative pronoun, like "who" or "which," that only makes sense when it helps to describe another noun in an independent clause:

which makes her feel sophisticated

That doesn't make sense on its own, but it does make sense when it's helping to explain how the duck feels about ordering a Pilsner:

She orders a Pilsner, which makes her feel sophisticated.

The dependent clause makes sense now because it is helping to explain — supporting — the idea about ordering a Pilsner. It explains what ordering a Pilsner does for the duck.

Sometimes an otherwise independent clause is enslaved by a word to like "because" or "when":

because **ducks** don't have money

when **the bartender** asks for money

If you remove "because" or "when," these dependent clauses make sense on their own. They become grammatical sentences, in other words. But with those words attached to the beginning of the clauses, the clauses only make sense when they are helping to explain why or when a verb happens:

The old bartender with the Grateful Dead tattoo is confused because ducks don't have money.

When the bartender asks for money, **the duck** tells him to put it on her bill.

The dependent clause "because ducks don't have money" now makes sense because it helps explain why the bartender is confused. The dependent clause "when the bartender asks for money" makes senses because it identifies the moment in this little drama when the duck delivers her hilarious punch line.

The Pronoun Wrinkle

The only wrinkle in these otherwise reliable definitions of independent and dependent clauses is pronouns. The subject of a grammatical sentence can be pronoun like "she" or "it," as in:

She orders a Pilsner.

She tells him to put it on her bill.

These are grammatical sentences, but on their own, they don't make much sense because we don't know who "she" is. That information came from the start of the joke when we learned that "she" refers back to "a duck." In the second sentence, we also don't know who "him" is because there's no mention here of the bartender. In the same sentence, we only know what "it" means because we see "a Pilsner" in the first sentence.

This is what pronouns do. They refer back to an earlier noun phrase so that we don't annoy readers by repeating the same noun phrase:

A duck walks into a bar.

A duck orders a beer.

When the bartender asks the duck for money, the duck tells the bartender to put the beer on the duck's bill.

Repeating the same noun phrase over and over distracts readers from your ideas. So pronouns step in to make your essays more effective and your jokes funnier. That's why the rule-makers allow pronouns to stand in as the fully accredited subjects of grammatical sentences even though those sentences sometimes fail to capture a complete thought entirely on their own.

Therefore, when you see that a pronoun is the subject of a sentence, you should give that sentence a pass on the makes-sense-on-its-own test — as long as the sentence otherwise makes sense on its own.

Types of Grammatical Sentences

There are many ways to structure grammatical sentences. We can't cover it all in this little book, but we can at least introduce the basics here, and you can get more particulars from your writing professor or your handbook of English grammar. There are three main types of sentences — simple, compound, and complex — and these types of sentences are defined by the sort of clauses that go into them.

The Simple Sentence

The simple sentence consists of one independent clause — one subject and one predicate — without any dependent clauses. Like this:

> **An elephant** walks into a bar.

> **He** thinks one thing.

> "**This bar** is really big."

Simple sentences can be also be long:

> **A young elephant with a serious drinking problem** walks very carefully into a bar in the afternoon on the first day of spring.

But there will always be one subject and one predicate and no dependent clauses. That's a pretty simple definition, so naturally there are some wrinkles here that you should be aware of.

The first wrinkle is that your subject can be a **compound subject**. This is a subject that joins two or more noun phrases joined together by a word like "and" or "or":

> **A string** (noun phrase 1) **and another string** (noun phrase 2) walk into a bar.

The two noun phrases become a unit, and the predicate describes what both are doing. You get a two-for-one with a compound subject — two subjects for one predicate.

The second wrinkle is that a predicate can be a **compound predicate**. As you might expect, this happens when two or more verb phrases are joined together with a word like "and" or "or":

> **The bartender** looks at the two (verb phrase 1) and tells them to leave (verb phrase 2).

> **The two strings** go outside (verb phrase 1), mess up their hair (verb phrase 2), tangle themselves together (verb phrase 3), and go back into the bar (verb phrase 4).

In the first example, the subject of the sentence ("the bartender") does two things. He looks. He tells. The word "and" joins those two verbs and their phrases together into a compound predicate. In the second sentence, the single subject does four things — go, mess up, tangle, and go — with "and" combining all four actions into a compound predicate. Impressive work by the predicate.

One last wrinkle with predicates is that there are two kinds of verbs to be aware of. In the example above, you have predicates tell you what the subject does ("walks," "looks," "tells," and so on). These are called **action verbs**. Predicates can also tell you what the subject is like with **linking verbs** such as "is" or "seems." These verbs link the subject to descriptive information. For example, when the bartender asks, "Weren't you just in here?" one string uses a linking verb to say:

I am a frayed knot.

Get it? Afraid not? In this case, "am" is the linking verb and "a frayed knot" is another noun phrase that describes the subject "I." The information that a linking verb connects to the subject in this way is called a **complement**. That won't be on the midterm, but I needed to talk about something while you were working out the punch line to that joke.

Compound Sentences

You've seen that word "compound" already with compound subjects and compound predicates. It can apply to independent clauses, too. When you join two or more independent clauses with a word like "and" or "or," the result is called a **compound sentence**. Compound sentences join independent clauses that are related and equally important ideas. The clauses each make sense when taken on their own.

I don't think you will be surprised to learn that there's a technical term for those words like "and" or "or." It's **coordinating conjunction**. The "conjunction" part describes the use of these words — to bring things together in the same way that a highway junction brings two roads together. The "coordinating" part shows that the two joined clauses are still equal and independent.

At some point, all English-speaking people are taught to memorize these coordinating conjunctions with the rather odd mnemonic "FANBOYS," which captures all seven coordinating conjunctions in one acronym that isn't really a word:

For And Nor But Or Yet So

In actual practice, however, you will probably only use "and," "or," "but," and "so." "For," "nor," and "yet" are starting to sound pretty old-fashioned these days.

Here's a chart that shows you how compound sentences use a coordinating conjunction (cc) to combine two or more equally important independent clauses to create a larger, two-part idea:

Independent Clause	*cc*	*Independent Clause*
A termite walks into a bar,	but	**no one** is tending the bar.
The termite flies over to a table,	and	**he** lands in front of a woman.
The woman looks at him,	so	**he** smiles and clears his throat.
The termite points to the bar,	and	**he** asks, "Is the bar tender here?"

Technically, you can join any two independent clauses with a coordinating conjunction, and the result will be a grammatical sentence. Even this is a grammatical compound sentence:

A termite walks into a bar, but **a duck** orders a Pilsner.

That is a grammatical sentence, but it doesn't make sense because the two ideas aren't closely related. You should avoid not making sense.

The Complex Sentence

A **complex sentence** is not necessarily all that complex, but it does contain at least one dependent clause. The complexity comes from joining two or more ideas together in a way that makes one idea the main idea and turns any other ideas into supporting ideas — dependent clauses.

Take these two ideas, for example:

> **A bear** is tired of stealing beer from campers.

> **A bear** walks into a bar.

If you think these two ideas are equally important, you could combine them as a compound sentence like this:

> **A bear** is tired of stealing beer from campers, so **he** walks into a bar.

However, if you think the walking into the bar is the more important idea, then a complex sentence makes more sense:

> **A bear** walks into a bar because he is tired of stealing beer from campers.

You no longer have two independent clauses that are linked as equals by a coordinating conjunction. Now there is just one main clause. The subject is "a bear," and the predicate is the rest of the sentence. That idea about the bear being tired of stealing is no longer independent. The word "because" turns it into a dependent clause that explains why the bear walks into the bar. It supports the main clause by giving us information about the verb "walks."

Consider these three independent clauses:

> **The bear** orders a beer.

> **The bartender** refuses.

> **This bar** only serves non-hibernating mammals.

If you combine these independent clauses with coordinating conjunctions, you begin to see the limitations of the compound sentences:

> **The bear** orders a beer, but **the bartender** refuses, for **this bar** only serves non-hibernating mammals.

You see how "for" sounds old fashioned? Anyway, this sentence is grammatical, but it becomes a little hard to follow because it makes all three ideas equal. That's not the situation at the bar. Back at the bar, the refusal is the most important idea, so it should be the main clause, and the other ideas should help to explain it as dependent clauses. A complex sentence makes more sense:

> When the bear orders a beer, **the bartender** refuses because this bar only serves non-hibernating mammals.

Now the subject of the main clause is "the bartender," and the other two clauses explain when he refuses and why. One of the dependent clauses from the predicate shifts to the left and comes before the subject. That doesn't make it the subject. It makes it an introduction to the main clause. I'll have more to say about that in the next chapter.

Words like "when" and "because" are called **subordinating conjunctions**. There's another technical term for you. This one *will* be on the midterm. Like coordinating conjunctions, subordinating conjunctions connect different ideas, but they do this in a way that subordinates one clause to another. In other words, they join clauses together by creating subordinates — servants — supporting clauses that will only make sense when they are helping to explain the main clause.

There are dozens of subordinating conjunctions out there, so there's no handy acronym like FANBOYS. Some subordinating conjunctions are short phrases instead of single words, too, and that only complicates the matter. However, we tend to use a handful of them much more than the rest:

Chronological	*Cause or Effect*	*Conditional*
after	because	if
until	since	even if
before	so that	although
when		even though
whenever		unless
while		

You'll notice that the ever popular "however" and "therefore" are not included here. That's because they aren't subordinating conjunctions. They're transitional words that connect one idea to not just one but several other ideas. When you use them, you just stick them into an existing sentence.

Another way to create complex sentences is with what is called a **relative pronoun**. These are special pronouns that combine ideas by relating one idea to a noun phrase in a previous idea. Consider these two independent clauses:

The bear points to a woman.

The woman is sitting at the bar.

The first independent clause presents the more important idea because this is a joke about a bear. The second clause only provides information about the woman in the first clause. It's the perfect situation for a complex sentence, the wedding of two unequal ideas, and a relative pronoun is a great way to do this:

The bear points to a woman who is sitting at the bar.

The resulting clause — "who is sitting at the bar" — no longer makes sense by itself. It's become a dependent clause, and it only makes sense when it's used to provide more information about a noun phrase in the main clause.

Like regular pronouns, relative pronouns require some other noun phrase to be introduced first. Unlike regular pronouns, relative pronouns have to follow immediately after that noun phrase. They don't stand on their own like "he" or "it" do. They have to be accompanied by a predicate that provides more information about the related noun phrase. Here are your relative pronouns and what they refer to:

Things	*People*	*People or Things*
which	who	that
	whom	whose

With these relative pronouns in mind, figure out which one you would use to combine these two independent clauses into a complex sentence:

The woman's left arm sported a bright red tattoo.

The tattoo said, "Bar Bitch!"

My guess is that you would choose either "that" or "which" to combine these two sentences. That's because the noun that both sentences have in common is "tattoo," a thing. If you didn't choose "that" or "which," then slap your forehead (not too hard) and use "that" to create a complex sentence:

The woman's left arm sported a bright red tattoo that said "Bar Bitch!"

Nice work, student writer. The less important idea is right where it belongs — in the supporting dependent clause.

There are reasons to choose "that" over "which" in this situation, and there are reasons to choose "which" over "that" in other situations. If you're at all curious, ask your writing professor. This is just the sort of question that is sure to make his day. And if you are curious but don't have a writing professor handy, then look up the terms "restrictive relative clauses" and "nonrestrictive relative clauses" in your handbook of English grammar or the Internet.

To illustrate how complex sentences work, here are some examples and explanations. I'll put the dependent clauses in [brackets] to make it easier to see how they are supporting the main clause:

Sentence	*Explanation*
"[If you don't serve me a beer], I will eat that woman [who has the tattoo]."	The first dependent clause is created by the subordinating conjunction "if." It presents a condition that, if present, will lead to the main clause happening.
	The second dependent clause is created by the relative pronoun "who." It provides information to identify the woman whom the bear threatens to eat.

[Even though he personally has no problem with bears], **the bartender** shakes his head [because he has to follow bar policies].	Both of these dependent clauses are created by subordinating conjunctions. The first one, "even though," introduces a qualification to the bartender's refusal. In the second one, the subordinating conjunction "because" introduces the reason why he still must refuse.
The bear then eats the woman, [who tastes a little like chicken].	The relative pronoun "who" refers to "the woman" and introduces some information that doesn't really have any anything to do with the joke.
[When the police [that the bartender calls] finally arrive], **they** quickly arrest the bear for drug abuse.	This one is a little tricky. The subordinating conjunction "when" introduces a dependent clause that tells us when the arrest took place. However, within that dependent clause, the relative pronoun "that" introduces a dependent clause that explains which police arrive. So you have a supporting clause that supports a supporting clause that supports the main clause. And you thought grammar was boring.
The bear can't believe his ears and asks them [why they're charging him with drug abuse].	That's right, student writers — a compound predicate! The subordinating conjunction "why" introduces a dependent clause that explains what the bear asks in the second verb phrase of that compound predicate.
"**We**'re arresting you for drug abuse [because that was the bar bitch you ate]."	In this one, you'll first of all notice that the subject is only half of the first word, a contraction for "we are." I thought I'd point that out. The dependent clause is created by the word "because" and explains why they are arresting the bear for drug abuse. It's also the punch line.

Get it? *Bar bitch you ate* — which sounds like "barbiturate" — which is a class of drugs that is often abused as recreational drugs.

Practice Makes Less Imperfect

Remember that this is just an introduction. The more important work of learning to use grammatical sentences will come as you begin to practice your new technical skills. That's when you begin to see how these rules work and why some sentences are grammatical and some are not.

You have two ways to practice these new skills — as a writer and as a reader.

Work on Grammar as a Writer

As a writer, the first way to work on grammar is to examine your sentences to see if each sentence follows the rules of grammar. You can do that by checking to see if each sentence makes sense — on its own — without relying on the sentence that comes before it or after it. That sounds easy enough, but it's actually pretty hard. Your brain has read all these sentences and knows exactly what you mean. The sentences sounded good to you when you wrote them, after all.

So try this trick — read the paper backwards, one sentence at a time. That breaks up the flow of ideas in the paper, so your brain will have an easier time analyzing whether there's a complete thought in any one sentence. We'll talk more about this and other tricks in chapter 12.

A second technique is a little harder — especially at first — but in the long run, it's more effective. In each sentence, identify the subject and predicate of the main clause. If it's a compound sentence, then identify the subjects and predicates in both of the independent clauses. This kind of analysis won't be easy to do at first. You'll be forced to guess a lot. So get some help from a writing tutor. With help, it won't take you very long to get the hang of spotting subjects and predicates. Once you get the hang of doing that, you will become a better judge of your own sentences and — looking ahead to the next chapter — you will also be able to start following the rules of formal punctuation.

A third, writerly technique for learning these rules is to only write sentences that you *know* are grammatical, sentences where you know what the subject is and you know what the predicate is. Write short and simple sentences, in other words — shorter and simpler than usual. This will feel like baby talk, of course, but if you can endure that for a paper or two, it's an effective way to learn these rules. It won't be long before you're writing longer and more complex sentences that you know follow the rules of grammar.

And finally, if you are in a writing class, study any grammar-related comments you get back on your papers. That can be challenging, I know. Nobody likes to focus on the negative. And because grammar rules are a new topic, they may also seem kind of boring. But that doesn't change the fact that you need to learn this stuff to be taken seriously. So pay attention, student writer. Make sure you understand both the problems you created and the solutions your professor suggested. If you don't get it, then ask your professor to explain in more detail. That's the only way to learn from that particular mistake.

Work on Grammar as a Reader

Whether or not you are in a writing classroom, learning the rules of English grammar will also mean owning a handbook of English grammar. If you're in a writing class, one has probably been assigned. Buy a copy for yourself and don't sell it back at the end of the term. If you're not in a writing class, then just about any handbook will do. Check out several at a bookstore or online and buy the one that seems most user-friendly for you.

A good handbook of English grammar captures all the sentence rules — not just these basic ones. As a reference book, it's indexed and organized, which should make it easy to find more detailed explanations and examples when you need them. And although technical terminology can be challenging by itself, that's also your key to getting more help. A handbook introduces the terminology you will need to search online for even more help.

Second, even if English is your first language, you will find a world of help online at various English as a Second Language (ESL) websites. These websites help to explain the rules of grammar to people who have no prior experience with English, and they do so with simple, clear explanations and lots of examples. Because so many students in English-speaking countries are taught to write informally, they have never been introduced to the rules of grammar. ESL websites are thus perfect for students who only have an informal relationship with English. So check those out as well. Read them until you get it.

If you've ever studied the grammar of a foreign language, studying the rules of English grammar won't be too hard. Subjects in German are just like subjects in English. Predicates in Spanish are a lot like predicates in English. The terms you learned then will apply, so reach back into your past and use them. It was painful enough to acquire them. You might as well.

The Big Ideas

This chapter introduces you to some terrific "walks into a bar" jokes and the basic rules for creating grammatical sentences in English. Here are the big ideas from this chapter:

1. Grammatical sentences are expected: Formal readers will judge you by your sentences. If you can explain yourself with grammatical sentences, those readers will judge you to be competent and intelligent. If you can't — or won't — they would judge you to be less competent and less intelligent than you probably are.

2. Technical terms: To understand the rules of English grammar, you also have to understand a few important technical terms:

- **clause:** a group of words that captures an idea. It captures an idea because it contains two vital ingredients — a subject and a predicate.

- **complex sentence:** an independent clause that includes at least one dependent clause.

- **compound predicate:** two or more verb phrases joined together by a coordinating conjunction.

- **compound sentence:** two or more independent clauses joined together by a coordinating conjunction.

- **compound subject:** two or more noun phrases joined together by a coordinating conjunction.

- **coordinating conjunction:** a word such as "and," "or," "so," or "but" that joins words, phrases, clauses, or sentences together. The "coordinating" part means that each item in the list is equal in importance and similar in nature.

- **dependent clause:** a clause that for one reason or another doesn't make sense entirely on its own. It only makes sense when it helps to explain the idea in an independent clause.

- **independent clause:** a clause that makes sense entirely on its own — also known as a grammatical sentence.

- **noun phrase:** a pronoun or a single noun or a main noun and any words or phrases that help to describe that noun.

- **predicate:** the main verb phrase in a clause. It either tells us what the subject does, or it describes the subject.

- **pronoun:** a word like "she" or "we" or "this" that refers back to an earlier noun phrase so that you won't annoy your readers by repeating the same noun phrase over and over.

- **relative pronoun:** special pronouns such as "who" and "which" that create dependent clauses by relating one idea to a noun phrase in a previous idea.

- **simple sentence:** a single independent clause without any dependent clauses.

- **subject:** the main noun phrase in a clause. It's the thing that the clause is talking about.

- **subordinating conjunction:** a word such as "if," "because," or "when" that joins two different ideas — clauses — by turning one clause into a supporting idea for an independent clause.

- **verb phrase:** one verb and any words or phrases or dependent clauses that help to explain that verb.

3. Types of sentences: A simple sentence is a single independent clause. A compound sentence consists of two or more equally important and logically related independent clauses that are joined together by a coordinating conjunction. A complex sentence consists of an independent clause and at least one supporting — or dependent — clause.

4. Using these ideas: Until you start to see how these ideas and technical terms apply to your own writing, they aren't worth much. So your real task here is not studying for a vocabulary test. It's thinking about these terms as you write and as you read. You can get help with this from a number of sources, including your writing professor, college tutoring services, and ESL websites.

5. Barbiturate joke: Hilarious!

Chapter 4
Grammatical Sentences Require Formal Punctuation

As you saw in the last chapter, informal sentences try to capture how you normally speak. For that reason, the punctuation of informal writing is mostly sound related. You use commas, to, create, small, pauses. You use periods. To create. Longer. Pauses. You use quotation marks to "add emphasis" to a word or phrase or to make your voice sound "ironic." You use ellipses to make your voice . . . trail . . . off . . . . That's what you do in e-mails and texts. That's what you probably did with the school papers of your wayward youth. That's fine.

With formal writing, however, punctuation is *never* used to imitate the sounds of spoken sentences. Never. It's only used to show readers how your sentences are structured so that your readers will more easily understand your ideas. For this to happen, you must follow the actual rules of formal punctuation instead of any sound-based "rules of thumb."

And listen, your grammar-checking software isn't good enough to solve this problem for you, either. It's just scanning your sentences for word patterns and guessing about where you might need a comma or period or semicolon. But it doesn't know the meaning of your sentences, so it doesn't know if that punctuation mark is really needed. To be a competent writer, you have to learn this for yourself. That's just how it is.

So a new day is dawning for you, student writer, a day of using punctuation as it was meant to be used. It's the first day of the rest of your formally punctuated life. To get you started, this chapter will introduce you to all the important punctuation marks. Some of this you already know. Some of this you don't. Some of this you think you know — because you've always gotten A's in English — but you're mistaken. Read it all carefully, and pay particular attention to the comma.

Ending Punctuation

As you've learned, sentences are groups of words that make sense on their own. They do this by 1) stating a complete thought, 2) asking a question, or 3) giving a command. With any sentence, you mark the beginning of a sentence with a capital letter, and you mark the end of a sentence with **ending punctuation** — a period (.), question mark (?), or exclamation point (!).

With informal writing, you can manipulate ending punctuation to change the sound of your sentence. For example, you can make your voice louder or more enthusiastic by adding several exclamation points:

I can't believe how much I love grammar!!!

Or you can add a tone of astonishment to you voice with multiple question marks:

Really???

You can use the ellipsis — which is not really ending punctuation — to make your voice trail off:

I didn't think it was wrong...

You can even abuse the ellipsis to make your voice *really* trail off into a sad, guilty sigh with a bunch of ellipses:

To love grammar.........

With formal writing, however, your goal is not to recreate the sound of a spoken sentence. The goal is to precisely explain an idea. To do that, you only use one period, one question mark, or — rarely — one exclamation point. You can use an ellipsis and a period at the end of a sentence, but only when that sentence is part of a direct quotation. More about that later.

The only exception to this rule is when you ask a rhetorical question and want to add emphasis to it. You can then use a question mark and exclamation mark together:

Is it wrong to love grammar?!

But that's the only exception.

The Comma

The most used and abused punctuation mark is the comma (,). And it's really not your fault, either, student writer, because for years your teachers have been telling you to abuse it. They've told you to "put a comma where you hear a pause," a rule of thumb that works for informal, sound-based writing but not for formal, idea-based writing.

The problem with this rule of thumb is that when you're writing, different pauses have different meanings. For some pauses, you need a period because the pause separates one sentence from another. For other pauses, you need a comma because the pause separates a phrase from the rest of the sentence. And for still other pauses, you shouldn't put *any* punctuation because that will confuse the meaning of the sentence. If you persist in putting commas where you hear pauses, you're going to screw up a lot of sentences.

Student writers cling to this rule of thumb more than any other. It's like that favorite concert T-shirt they refuse to throw away even though the band broke up eight years ago and the shirt smells like mice have been at it, which they have. It has to go, student writer. It belongs to the past. It makes you look bad. Instead of putting commas where you hear pauses, you need to learn the actual rules for using commas so that your sentences make better sense.

Here's where you start — commas separate. They separate things within your sentence. Every comma rule explains a different way to separate the parts of your sentence so that readers can more easily understand your idea. Now we'll look at those rules.

1. Commas separate three or more items in a list

Put a comma after every item in your list except for the last one. Then use a coordinating conjunction (cc) prior to the last item to tie the list together.

Here's how the rule works as a formula:

item, item, {item, etc.} **cc** item

And here's how it works in this partial retelling of a classic joke:

So this bear <u>walks into a bar</u>, <u>sits down on a stool</u>, **and** <u>orders a beer</u>. (a list of verb phrases that form a compound predicate)

<u>The bartender</u>, <u>a policeman</u>, **and** <u>a woman</u> all look at the bear. (a list of noun phrases that form a compound subject)

The <u>wise</u>, <u>old</u>, **but** <u>unreflective</u> bartender tells the bear to get lost. (a list of adjectives that describe the noun "bartender")

The bear <u>angrily</u>, <u>hastily</u>, **and** <u>thirstily</u> rises from his stool and warns the bartender that he will eat the woman if the bartender doesn't give him a beer. (a list of adverbs that explain the verb "rises")

<u>With firmness</u>, <u>with clarity</u>, **and** <u>with a punch to the bear's nose</u>, the bartender refuses. (a list of prepositional phrases that explain the verb "refuses")

The bear then eats the woman <u>because the bartender refuses to comply with his demand</u>, <u>because the bear is angry about the punch in the nose</u>, and <u>because he has the impression that no one in the bar is taking him seriously as a bear</u>. (a list of dependent clauses that explain the verb "eats")

There are two things to notice with these sentences.

First, the lists are always groups of the same type of word or phrase (noun phrases, verbs, adjectives, and so on). If you create a list of items and one of them is not the same type of word or phrase, it will stick out oddly for your readers. They will notice that one of these things is not like the others, and that will distract them from your idea.

Second, notice that a comma goes after the item right before the coordinating conjunction. Some of you may have been taught to omit this comma, which goes by the name "Oxford comma," or "serial comma," or "the penultimate comma." That was the case when I was an impressionable young lad with my dreams of becoming an orthodontist, but times have changed. The convention now — for reasons too obscure for you or anyone else to worry about — is to use the <u>Oxford</u>, <u>serial</u>, **or** <u>penultimate</u> comma.

If you have a professor who says to omit it, then of course omit it. That professor is old and probably closer to the grave than you think. We want his or her death to be a happy one, so play along. However, after you are done with that ancient teacher, resume using this comma.

2. Commas separate two or more independent clauses within a compound sentence

This rule is much like Rule 1, where commas separate items in a list and a coordinating conjunction (cc) ties the list all together. However, with compound sentences, you use commas even when there are only two independent clauses in your list.

Here's how it looks as a formula:

Independent clause, {independent clause, etc.} **cc** independent clause.

Here's how it works in this partial retelling of a classic joke:

A bear walks into a bar, **and** it orders a beer.

The bartender tells the bear to get lost, **but** the bear warns the bartender that he will eat a woman at the bar if he doesn't get a beer.

The bartender still refuses, **so** the bear eats the woman.

The bartender calls the police, **and** they arrest the bear for drug abuse.

3. Commas separate interruptions from the main clause

In chapter 3, we talked about main clauses and the dependent clauses who love them. Dependent clauses provide information about the main clause, so they aren't considered interruptions. This rule only applies to words or phrases that interrupt an otherwise unified sentence with nonessential information or transitions to prior sentences. You might, for example, interrupt a sentence to add a transitional phrase like "for example." When you do this, you put a comma at the beginning and end of the interruption.

Here's how it looks as a formula:

Main, interruption, clause.

There are many, many types of interruptions that require this rule, and that variety makes the rule more difficult to master than the first two. But are you scared of a little complexity, student writer? Of course not! So here are a few of your options and some examples that will illustrate how this rule applies to the actual sentences of this partial retelling of a classic joke:

1. Appositives are words or phrases that rename a noun phrase. They only make sense when they come immediately after that noun:

> A bear, Smokey, walked into a bar and ordered a beer.

2. Asides are brief comments from the writer that provide extra information or commentary about the main clause as a whole:

> The bartender, like so many people, did not like bears and frowned at Smokey. (In this aside, the writer notes that this bartender was not alone in his dislike of bears. It's not a part of the main idea.)

> Smokey, alas, cared only about getting his beer. (This aside notes the writer's sadness about Smokey's drinking problem — also not part of the main idea.)

3. Transitions are words or phrases that tell the reader how this sentence is connected to other sentences in your writing, or maybe how this sentence fits into an organizational pattern:

> Smokey, therefore, ignored the frown and now demanded a beer.

> The bartender, in response, told Smokey to get out of the bar.

4. Negations are words or phrases that briefly state the opposite of a word or phrase in order to highlight the importance of that part of your main clause. The immediate contrast gives extra emphasis to the original word or phrase:

> Smokey is enraged, not intimidated, by the bartender.

5. Attributions are words or phrases that briefly identify the source of a quotation or idea — or possibly state that this is something you think or believe as the writer.

> Smokey, according to the police report, then threatens to eat a woman at the bar if he was not served a beer.

> The bartender, the report goes on to say, still refuses.

6. Direct address talks directly to the reader. This is used only with informal writing, but informal writing should be correctly punctuated, too:

So Smokey, <u>my dear student writers</u>, eats the woman.

7. Participial clauses are another type of dependent clause. They have this technical name because they are built around the "participle" form of a verb. This is either the –ing form (present tense, as in, "I am learn*ing* so many new terms.") or the –ed form (past tense, as in, "I wish I had learn*ed* these terms in fifth grade."). These clauses usually interrupt the main cause to add more information about the subject:

> The police, <u>responding to the bartender's phone call</u>, quickly arrived on the scene.

> Smokey, <u>covered by blood</u>, was the obvious suspect.

8. Relative clauses are like participial clauses, but they are trickier because you have to decide whether they interrupt the main clause or provide essential supporting information. If you decide they interrupt the main clause, they're called **nonrestrictive relative clauses** — there's a term that will impress your friends — and follow this rule. If you decide they provide essential supporting information to the main clause, then they are called **restrictive relative clauses** and do not follow this rule.

Here's what it looks like in practice:

> The police officer <u>who arrested Smokey</u> charged him with drug abuse. (This relative clause is restrictive because "who arrested Smokey" tells us which officer charged the bear, and that helps to explain the main clause. Rule 3 does not apply.)

> Smokey, <u>who can't believe the charge</u>, objects. (This relative clause is nonrestrictive because it does not provide essential supporting information about what happens in this main clause. Rule 3 applies.)

There's more to be said about relative clauses, of course, and your writing professor — or the Internet — or your handbook of English grammar — would love to talk with you about it.

One side issue with this rule is that interruptions can also come at the end of the main clause. When that happens, you put a comma before the interruption and only ending punctuation at the end of it:

Smokey objects to the charge, <u>which makes no sense to him</u>. (nonrestrictive relative clause)

It makes no sense to many listeners, <u>of course</u>. (aside)

That's just how jokes like this work, <u>however</u>. (transition)

4. Commas separate introductory words or phrases from the subject of the main clause

As writers, we often introduce the main clause with a word or phrase of transition or context. When we do that, we separate that introduction from the main clause with a comma. This rule is a cousin to Rule 3 because many of the interruptions listed there — transitions, direct addresses, asides, and participial clauses — can also be used as introductions to the main clause.

Here's how it looks as a formula:

<u>Introduction</u>, main clause.

Here's how it works in the sentences of this classic joke:

<u>In a completely different bear joke</u>, a bear walks into a bar. (prepositional phrase)

<u>With great concentration</u>, the bear very slowly asks for a "gin and —" (prepositional phrase)

<u>Because of his professional training</u>, the bartender waits patiently for the rest of the order. (dependent clause)

<u>However</u>, the bear does not immediately finish the sentence. (transition)

<u>In all honesty</u>, it seems like the sentence will never end. (aside)

<u>Finally</u>, the bear concludes with "tonic." (transition)

<u>With visible relief</u>, the bartender agrees and pours the drink. (prepositional phrase)

<u>Trying to be friendly</u>, the bartender then asks the bear what the deal was with the big pause. (participial clause)

"<u>Alas</u>, I was born with them." (aside)

Get it? Big pause. Big paws. There's a reason they say that the pun is the highest form of humor. Anyway, you have two side issues to keep in mind.

First, it's common to have more than one introduction before the subject of the main clause. When that happens, each introduction gets its own comma:

> Finally, after two minutes, while the rest of the patrons look on, the bear concludes with "tonic." (transition, prepositional phrase, dependent clause)

Second, this rule usually does *not* apply to adverbs that come before the subject of the sentence. This is especially true if the adverbs are time-related adverbs:

> Now the bartender simply waits for the rest of the order.

> Then the bear says the word "tonic."

Why do adverbs get away with this sort of thing? Because adverbs are slippery fish. They live carefree lives. They can insert themselves just about anywhere in a sentence without requiring commas. We all know people who get away with anything. Adverbs are like those people. I don't know how they get away it. They just do.

5. Commas separate direct quotations from attributions

This is a rule that needs more explanation than you're going to get for now. One issue is that this is only one way to introduce a direct quotation, and the other ways don't use commas. Second, this rule interacts with a lot of other punctuation rules. Sometimes a comma is involved, and sometimes it isn't. We'll start with the basics here, but you should keep thinking about this as you continue on to learn about colons and quotation marks.

Here's how this rule looks as a formula:

> Identifying statement, "Direct quotation."

> "Direct quotation," identifying statement.

Here's how it works in the sentences of this classic joke about a horse that walks into a bar:

"I'd like a beer," says the horse.

The bartender says, "Okay, but why the long face?"

6. Commas separate the parts of multi-part nouns

This is the most superficial of the comma rules. It exists mostly for visual clarity when you present large numbers, full dates, and the official names of things that have more than one part to them. These commas help readers to keep the information straight with these multi-part nouns.

Here's how:

Numbers

Use commas to separate most large numbers into groups of three digits.

My mother has 1,000 chins.

Your mother has 1,000,000 chins.

Places

Use a comma to separate contextual information that is closely related to a place name — city and state, city and country, state and country, and so on.

My mother moved to Paris, Texas.

I wish she had moved to Paris, France, instead.

People

Separate the name of a person from any titles, degrees, or other suffixes that follow that name. If there is more than one, separate each one with commas.

Kurt Vonnegut, Jr., is the son of Kurt Vonnegut, Sr.

Vonnegut used to drink beer with Wallace Stegner, PhD.

Dates

When offering the full date and event, separate the year and other information from the rest of the date with commas.

I was born on May 14, 1960.

May 15, 1960, would have been fine.

However, *don't* use a comma if you only give the month and the year.

> May 1960 was quite a long time ago.

The Colon

The colon (:) introduces an idea or list or direct quotation. It's like an equals sign from the math side of your brain. On the left side is a statement — an independent clause — and on the right side are either some details that illustrate that statement or another independent clause that clarifies it.

Here's how it looks as a formula:

> **Statement**: details or clarification.

Here's how it works in this partial retelling of a classic joke:

> **The beginning of the joke focuses on the bear**: "A bear walks into a bar." (direct quotation)

> **The bear then makes himself at home**: sitting on a bar stool, looking at the menu, and ordering a beer. (list of participial phrases)

> **The bartender is not friendly**: he has a lot of baggage regarding bears that trace back to an unfortunate vacation at Yellowstone National Park. (another independent clause)

The colon will be useful to you in formal writing, where it frequently introduces direct quotations. As you use it, however, keep this in mind: the statement on the left side of the colon *must* be an independent clause. The details on the right side of the colon can be a direct quotation, a list, or another independent clause. It just has to illustrate or clarify the statement on the left side.

There is some debate about whether to capitalize an independent clause on the right side of the right side of the colon. Unless it's a direct quotation, I say no. If this is something that interests you, talk to your writing professor. Ask about the interrobang while you're at it. Then look into the requirements for earning an English degree.

You're clearly one of us.

Quotation Marks

In formal writing, quotation marks (" ") have two uses, and they're both important. The first and most important use is to show the beginning (") and end (") of a direct quotation — a word-for-word transcription of someone else's writing or speech. This is important because in formal writing, you're expected to take great care in separating what you've written from what others have written or said. You have to give credit to those others, and you can't do that if the reader can't tell what you're borrowing and what you wrote yourself.

With a quoted word or phrase, quotation marks show the beginning and ending of the quotation, and no other punctuation is required:

> The police arrested the bear for "drug abuse."

If what you are quoting is a full sentence, then you must also introduce the sentence. This means adding a comma when you identify the source in your introduction or a colon if your introduction summarizes or interprets the quotation:

> The horse says, "I'd like a beer, please."

> The bartender responds with compassion: "Okay, but why the long face?"

You do get that joke, right? Anyway, the second use of quotation marks in formal writing is to discuss a word as a word. For example, if I were to write about the word "bear," I would talk about how "bear" has many meanings, most of which have nothing to do with large, ferocious mammals. I would be talking about the word, not actual bears. The quotation marks indicate that the focus is on the word only.

Single quotation marks (' ') are used when a direct quotation contains quotation marks of its own. Suppose, for example, that this is the original sentence that you are quoting:

> The police arrested the bear for "drug abuse."

If you were to quote this joke in a paragraph of your own, you would use single quotation marks to replace the double quotation marks in the original:

> Humble uses this extremely effective sentence to illustrate the use of commas with introductory phrases: "The police arrested the bear for 'drug abuse.'"

With informal writing, there's the practice of using quotation marks to make a statement sound ironic:

> My hair looks "really great" this morning.

This puts air quotes around "really great," so that others know you mean the opposite of "really great" — and that you're fishing for compliments or sympathy. Don't do that with formal writing. You can still be ironic within formal writing but you have to be subtler than that, my friend. And your hair looks fine, by the way.

Driving around town, you might also see quotation marks used informally to add emphasis to a phrase. For some reason, this happens a lot in ads:

> All inventory "half off"!

> Special "buy one, get one" sale!

> "Fresh" apples!

But that's an abuse of quotation marks, even for informal writing. It makes the writer look dumb.

One side issue to keep in mind is that this is how quotation marks work with American English. With British English, writers use single quotation marks where Americans use doubles and double quotation marks where Americans use singles. The British also say "biscuit" where Americans say "cookie." This is just something to keep in mind in case you have to quote a British writer or a British writer offers you a "biscuit."

There are other side issues to learn about with quotation marks and direct quotations — especially when it comes to how they interact with other punctuation marks. Does the comma come before the ending quotation mark? Does it come after? For the particulars, you'll need to read further in your handbook of English grammar.

The Ellipsis

The ellipsis (...) has a very precise use. It shows readers that unnecessary words have been omitted within a direct quotation. Suppose this is the full direct quotation:

> You are the most disappointing child that a mother could imagine, and a mother can imagine a pretty disappointing child.

With the ellipsis, you can omit the unnecessary words to boil this quotation down to its bare essentials:

> You are... a pretty... child.

If the omission comes at the end of the sentence, or if the omission stretches over more than one sentence, you add a fourth period to show that the end of at least one sentence has also been omitted:

> You are... pretty....

One side issue to keep in mind is that you should only do this to remove unnecessary or less important information so that readers can focus on the main point. You shouldn't use the ellipsis to change the meaning of the main clause like I just did. I guess this is one of those "do as I say, not as I do" moments.

If you have used the ellipsis in the past, it was probably to create the sound of your voice trailing off in an e-mail or tweet or online post:

> I just don't know...

Or maybe you used it to create a sense of anguish in a poem:

> love...
>   pain...
>   you...........

That's fine with informal writing and gut-wrenching poetry, but it has no place in formal writing, so knock it off.

The Apostrophe

The apostrophe is important to figure out because when you misuse it, you look particularly bad — especially to others who have managed to figure it out first. They overgeneralize about it. Instead of saying, "Look — this goofball doesn't know how to use the apostrophe," they say, "Look at this goofball!"

The misuse happens mostly when the apostrophe is used in combination with the letter "s," and it happens because the correct use of the apostrophe sounds the same as the misuse. Untangling this confusion will take a little time, so be patient as I lay it out for you. Once you see that, you'll be able to make a much better impression on your readers.

Contractions

A contraction is really a *sub*traction. You subtract letters from a word or two to create a shorter word, and you use an apostrophe to show readers that letters have been subtracted from that word:

I am = I'm	they are = they're
I would or I had = I'd	they have = they've
I have = I've	they had = they'd
you are = you're	do not = don't
she is or she has = she's	does not = doesn't
it is or it has = it's	will not = won't
we are = we're	let us = let's

You also use an apostrophe when you subtract letters or numbers from the start of a word — "'tis the season," "I don't remember '69 very well," and so on.

At some point in your educational career, some English teacher probably told you this: "Never use contractions." Here is one time when your English teacher was talking about formal instead of informal writing. It's a general expectation that you should not use contractions in formal writing. I'm not sure why this is expected, but it is, so send a thank you note to that particular English teacher and follow his or her advice.

Possessive Nouns

A possessive noun is a noun phrase that's been transformed by an apostrophe — and various spellings of the "s" sound — into a kind of adjective that helps to describe another noun in a new noun phrase.

Here's what it looks like in practice:

noun phrase	*possessive noun + [noun]* *= new noun phrase*
Bob	Bob's [nose]
the dog	the dog's [nose]
the rockets	the rockets' [red glare]
the children	the children's [noses]

That looks easy enough, but it gets complicated because the apostrophe and "s" sound are used in different ways for different types of noun phrases. Here's a quick run-through of all your options:

Singular Nouns

If the noun phrase is singular — it consists of only one thing — then add an apostrophe and "s" to the end of it, even if the singular noun already ends in an "s."

noun phrase	*possessive noun + [noun]* *= new noun phrase*
the dog	the dog's [nose]
James	James's [nose]

Back in the day, you didn't add an "s" after an apostrophe if the singular noun ended in an "s." You may still run into a teacher or two who assert that this is still the case. That's fine. You already understand that these kind, elderly teachers who are living in the past. There is no need for you to wake them from that lovely dream. Just do what they require while you are working with them, but don't let it become a habit, or else you too will be living in the past.

Plural Nouns That End in "s"

If the original noun phrase is plural — it consists of more than one thing — and if it ends in an "s," as most plural nouns do, then add just an apostrophe after the "s." Do not add a second "s."

noun phrase	possessive noun + [noun] = new noun phrase
the rockets	the rockets' [red glare]
the foxes	the foxes' [noses]
the Joneses	the Joneses' [house]

Plural Nouns That Don't End in "s"

If the noun phrase is plural and does not end in an "s" — and there are a lot of plural words in English that operate like this — then add an apostrophe and an "s" at the end of the word.

noun phrase	possessive noun + [noun] = new noun phrase
the children	the children's [noses]
most people	most people's [noses]

Pronouns

Finally, you do *not* use apostrophes to create possessive pronouns. Possessive pronouns are separate words that have different spellings, so you just use the right possessive pronoun and its existing spelling.

Here are the regular pronouns and their possessive cousins:

regular	*possessive*
I	my
you	your
he	his
she	her
it	its
we	our
they	their

And here are the relative pronouns and their possessives:

relative	*possessive*
that	whose
which	whose
who	whose

Possessive pronouns make a lot of student writers look bad. That's because most of them sound the same as other words — "your," "its," and "their," for example, sound identical to "you're," "it's," and "there" or "they're." The problem is that these words have very different meanings. Spelling doesn't matter when you're talking, of course, but it matters when you're writing. You have to spell the word that means the right thing or else you look like you don't know the difference.

We'll spend more time with that in chapter 5. For now, just remember that possessive pronouns never use apostrophes. There are thankfully no exceptions to this exception to the apostrophe rule.

Plurals of Single Letters

The most insignificant of the apostrophe rules is paradoxically one that causes a lot of apostrophe-related heartache. You can create a plural noun with an apostrophe and an "s," but only when the noun is a single letter and only when the "s" would otherwise create a different word or confuse the reader. Consider these two insightful sentences:

> There are three bs in "Bobby."

> As an honor student, I earn straight As.

The "bs" in the first sentence is distracting because "bs" means something other than "two or more of the letter b." In the second sentence, the "s" creates the word "as," which is not the intended meaning. In this case, and in this case only, you can use an apostrophe with the "s" to improve the clarity of the meaning:

> There are three b's in "Bobby."

> As an honor student, I earn straight A's.

If you're writing about single letters, then go ahead and use the apostrophe with your "s." Otherwise, never use an apostrophe to create a plural noun. Don't use an apostrophe with plural numbers, for example. Just use the "s":

> She was born in the 1970s.

> We played Crazy 8s until 2 in the morning.

Don't use an apostrophe with plural acronyms. Just use the "s":

> I own six PCs and 100 DVDs and 250 CDs.

Don't use an apostrophe with the plural form last names, either. Just use the "s," and if the last name ends with an "s," just use "es" like you would with any other noun:

> Last night we visited the Humbles.

> The Joneses were not at home.

In summary, then, with every plural noun except for single letters, don't use an apostrophe. Just use the "s" or "es" or "ies" — however the dictionary tells you to spell the plural form. I don't care how you see the apostrophe used in advertising, at farm stands, and on those wooden plaques that tell you whose house you're visiting. Follow the actual rules and not those bad examples.

Punctuation You Shouldn't Use

With formal writing, there are some punctuation marks that you should avoid until your punctuation skills are much more developed, and there are some that you should avoid entirely and forever. Here's a quick look at that.

The Semicolon

The semicolon (;) is the darling of grammar checkers, the most popular of the bad guesses they will offer you. Always say no those guesses, even if they are occasionally correct. Semicolons should only be used by trained professionals, and even trained professionals should understand that they look just a little pretentious for doing so.

Back in the day — say 200 years ago — the typical English sentence was much longer. Jane Austen could crank out a 300-word sentence as easily as you or I now text our loved ones to bring home pizza. With a 300-word sentence, the comma is not sufficient to separate the various sub-units because there are so many sub-units and because some of those sub-units also have commas embedded within them. With a 300-word sentence, the semicolon gets called in as a kind of super-comma to separate introductions and interruptions that have commas embedded within them. Commas within commas! However, the last time anyone actually wrote a 300-word sentence was in June of 1908, so enough with the semicolons.

Today, there are only two necessary uses for the semicolon, so learn them well and reject all other possibilities.

The first is to make a winking smiley face:

;-)

However, you can only do that with informal writing. It is frowned upon in the formal paper.

The second necessary use for the semicolon is to create list of items that have commas embedded within them, and I can only think of two lists that do that — lists of cities and lists of dates:

> I have lived in Portland, Oregon; Santa Cruz, California; **and** Mason Butte, Idaho.

> You told me to get a job on March 3, 1988; March 8, 1988; **and** March 12, 1988.

With lists like this, you can use semicolons. But unless you are a trained professional — or Jane Austen — that's *it* for semicolons.

The Dash

The dash (—) is should almost never be used in formal writing. If you want to learn more about it, I won't stop you. You can read all about it in your handbook of English grammar or on the Internet. But don't use it in your formal papers, student writer, unless you know what you're doing. If you *don't* know what you're doing, your use of those dashes will make that abundantly clear to your reader.

Smiley Faces, Winking or Otherwise

No.

How to Learn Everything Else

This is just a starting point. There is much more to learn, and as I have said a few times too many, your best resource for learning punctuation is a good handbook of English grammar. That will cover all the rules for all the punctuation and provide many examples. If that's not enough, ask the Internet for more. Search for "comma rules" or whatever other rules you are trying to figure out. Some sites will have better explanations and illustrations than others, but they will all pretty much agree about what the rules are.

If you're in a writing class, you can also get help from your writing professor. Some of this help may be forced upon you in the form of high-lighted punctuation errors. Pay attention to that. You will find that there are probably three or four punctuation rules that you personally break a lot, and if you can figure those out, you will be mostly okay.

And listen, if the feedback you're getting from your professor isn't sufficient for your desire to learn punctuation, ask for more. Your professor won't believe you're really asking for more, so ask twice so that she will know that you are not part of a wish-fulfillment dream. That could get weird in a hurry.

As you continue to write college papers — and later, as you write within whichever professional livelihood you pursue — keep going back to your handbook. In doing that, the rules will become a more automatic part of writing for you. You will no longer guess about how your sentences should be written. You will decide.

Why This Book Doesn't Follow Its Own Advice

This is now the fourth chapter you've read about the form of formal writing. By now, you have probably noticed that the sentences in this book break many of the rules from all of these chapters. A lot of the paragraphs are formed to make the page look easy to read. There are sentence fragments all over the place. Here, for example. And I use many — *many* — dashes. What's the deal with that?

The deal is that most student writers don't tend to read writing text-books that are written in a formal style. Given the choice between reading a formal textbook and some other chore — say unloading the dishwasher — they'll unload that dishwasher nine times out of ten, even if they were the ones who loaded it in the first place.

And unfortunately, most writing textbooks are written in a formal style. That's so that the people who order the books — mostly professors — will see that the textbook writers are not just teachers of formal writing but have also mastered formal writing themselves. They want their books to earn the respect of their peers so that their peers will order a million copies of their books.

But I have no reputation to protect. I barely have a job. I just want you to read this book. I want you to learn the basics about formal writing so that you can unclench whenever it's time to write the next college essay. So I write to you in a conversational style. I use everyday language that you are willing to read, and I throw in a few outstanding bear jokes to close the deal. And that is why I shameless break my own rules. It's all for you, student writer.

You'll see how this continues to play out in the next chapter, too, when we take a closer look at the words that go into your sentences. My choice of words is shockingly informal.

The Big Ideas

This chapter introduced you to formal punctuation — punctuation that follows conventional rules and that is used to make your meaning clear to readers. Here are the big ideas from this chapter:

1. Informal versus formal punctuation: Informal punctuation uses punctuation... marks... to recreate, the, "sound" of your voice. Formal punctuation uses punctuation marks to show readers the structure — and thus the meaning — of your sentence. Informal punctuation is sound based. Formal punctuation is meaning-based.

2. The comma: You must never again put a comma where you hear a pause. You must never again put a comma where you hear a pause. You must never again put a comma where you hear a pause. You must never again put a comma where you hear a pause. You must never again put a comma where you hear a pause. You must never again put a comma where you hear a pause. You must never again put a comma where you hear a pause. Seriously — follow the comma rules instead.

3. The apostrophe: This tiny punctuation mark makes you look bad when you misuse it, and it's easy to misuse because it doesn't change the sound of a word. This means you need to stop guessing or doing what you see from the informal writers in your life. Just learn the rules for how to use the apostrophe correctly. It's not *that* hard.

Chapter 5

Sentences Are Made of Carefully Chosen Words

As you saw in the chapters about paragraphs and sentences, formal writing has higher expectations than what you are probably used to as an informal writer. As you already suspect, student writer, it's the same thing with the words you use. Formal writing expects you to choose your words carefully and spell them correctly.

Formal writing always has a job to do, so every word counts. If a word helps to get the job done, it counts in a positive way. If it distracts from that job, then it counts in a negative way. Any incorrect word choices or misspellings distract from the job at hand, so they count against you. And even if you have brilliant ideas, using the wrong "there" will make you look less intelligent to your reader, and that takes some of the shine off your ideas.

In this chapter, we'll look at how to make your words count in a positive way. That mostly means accuracy. Partly it means professionalism. Partly it means spelling. We'll start with the basic stuff — the things that you must do in order to not embarrass yourself. Then we'll look at ways to take accuracy to the next level and help to improve the quality of your thinking. We'll end with a long and somewhat nerdy look at common word-choice errors and how to avoid them.

Choose the Right Word

The easiest way to improve the accuracy of your writing is simply to choose the right word for what you mean. For example, if you want to thank the scholarship committee for the time they are taking to review your application, you have to thank them for "their time" — not "there time" or "they're time" or "their thyme." If you don't use "their time," then you're probably wasting *your* time.

How do you know whether to use "their" or "there" or "they're"?

You look up your options in a dictionary.

But how can people be expected to look up words that they don't know how to spell? It's inhumane.

I have complained the same thing myself, student writer, and I was complaining because I didn't want to do any actual work. The answer to the question is pretty simple, though. You *guess* at the spelling by how it sounds, and if that doesn't work, then you guess again — and again — until you find it. It's not that hard to do.

The real problem here is motivation. To choose the right word, all you really need is enough motivation to get off your intellectual butt and make the effort to use a dictionary. It doesn't take that long. You just have to care enough about the paper to do a good job with it.

And not to get too sidetracked, but sooner or later you will figure out that every college paper you write is worth caring about. The superficial reason to care is that it's going to be judged — graded — and part of the grade will be based on how professional your work is. The deeper and lasting reason to care is that each paper is here to teach you something. The more you care about that, the easier it will be to care about your papers.

Spell Your Words Correctly

Another basic expectation is that all your words are spelled correctly.

With conversation, all you have to do is make sounds. You don't need to know that "baby" is a four-letter word. You can think it's spelled "baybee" and be fine because all your listeners need is the "bay" and the "bee."

Informal writing is not quite as forgiving as actual conversation, but because it mimics the sound of spoken language, it's still pretty forgiving when it comes to spelling and word choice. A phrase like "one for all" can be "one 4 all," and nobody really cares. The sound of "for" is what matters most.

But with formal writing, correct spelling matters. It's not optional. And worse still, formal readers will use spelling to judge your intelligence. The judgment is fairly straightforward — if their spelling is better than yours, they will think that they are smarter than you. You do that. I do that. Everybody does that. So that's one more reason to take spelling seriously.

But I don't have to learn how to spell, say so many student writers, because I have software for that.

Foolish student writers!

Spelling-check software can only make educated guesses about misspelled words. It doesn't know what meaning you have in mind for that misspelled word, so if it finds a misspelling, the best it can

> **"Spelling-check software can only make educated guesses about misspelled words.... It doesn't know which suggestion is correct. It doesn't know if *any* of them is correct. In other words, it's stupid."**

do is notify you with a squiggly red line and offer some suggestions. And why is there usually more than one suggestion? Because your spell checker doesn't know which suggestion is correct. It doesn't know if *any* of them is correct. In other words, your spell checker is stupid.

Consider the misspellings in this sentence:

Captain Ahab's spetial harpoon never pierced the grate wite wale.

For the misspelled word "spetial," my spell checker alerts me to the misspelling with squiggly red line and offers two guesses — "spatial," the first or recommended word, and "special." If I were to trust my spell checker's recommendation, that word "spatial" would describe the harpoon as "three-dimensional." Most harpoons are three-dimensional, so I don't need "spatial" to describe that. However, if I want to distinguish this particular harpoon from the others on board, I need to use the word "special." Only Captain Ahab got to use that *baybee*.

The misspelled word "wite" is also a challenge for my poor, stupid spell checker. My spell checker offers five guesses — "white," "write," "wide," "wit," and "wife." It suggests "white" as the top choice, which is good because that's the word I need to describe the color of this large aquatic mammal. However, those other four guesses tell me that my spell checker doesn't feel great about that top guess. It adds the other guesses just in case. Again, if I want to be sure about which guess to use, I need to look up my options in a dictionary and pick the correct one.

An even larger problem with trusting spell checkers is that they can only tell you about the *mis*spelled words. Because they don't know the meaning of your sentence, they can't tell you if you are using a correctly spelled but wrong word. This leads to all sorts of goofy errors that make you look bad.

In the Captain Ahab sentence, for example, the words "grate" and "wale" are spelled correctly, but they don't mean "massive" or "large aquatic mammal," as my idea requires. "Grate" means "grill," "irritate," or "shred." "Wale" means "a ridge on a textured woven fabric such as corduroy." If I don't fix this, the noun phrase will mean an irritating piece of corduroy and not the large aquatic mammal I have in mind.

If you struggle with spelling and have a hard time learning the spelling of new words, you might consider getting some extra help. If you're enrolled in college, your college probably offers supplemental classes or workshops that focus on spelling. Whether you're in college or not, many books also help with spelling. A lot of people struggle with spelling, so there are a lot of helpful books out there. Take a look at some books, and pick one or two that you think look useful.

Be Professional

Because formal writing is always used within a professional context — between you and a professor, judge, boss, or hiring committee — your readers expect you to be professional and much less personal than you would be if you were talking to your friends. They don't want your word choice to draw attention away from that.

Consider this paragraph:

> Nowadays it sucks to be a student because there's never any way to make it happen without taking out TONS of student loans. My dad got

GRANTS to go to school back in the day, free money, money he didn't even NEED, really, and his parents gave him money, too. Well, going to school now means basically taking out a mortgage on my LIFE. Is that fair? No way!

If we look just at the observation and its short bit of evidence, this is a reasonable enough opinion. For this student, going to school requires thousands of dollars in student loan debt. Compared to the public support that was available to the student's father, the student is in a far worse situation. However, that's not what you notice about this paragraph. You notice the CAPITAL LETTERS, the conversational whining, and the word "sucks."

This approach is not uncommon for student writers. Wanting to connect with readers, they work hard to *not* show off their intelligence by *not* using professional language and grammatical sentences. Instead, they translate their complex ideas into an informal, conversational style.

Foolish student writers!

Your formal readers are trying to understand your ideas, so you must focus on your ideas, too. You must remove your distracting capital letters. You must remove distracting conversational habits — like starting sentences with "Well" or "Anyhow." You must replace distracting informal words like "sucks" and "nowadays" with precise, conventional words like "is costly" and "today."

You should also avoid inflammatory words. Swear words, for example, are almost never credible in the college essay. Vulgarity rarely works. You know that, though. A more common mistake is to present your ideas with words that make fun of topics or ideas that are important to your readers. In doing that, you make fun of your readers, too, even if you do so with professional language.

Consider these three topic sentences for the same paragraph:

Senate Bill 211 could have the unintended consequence of raising the infant mortality rate in our state.

Senate Bill 211 is a threat to children.

Senate Bill 211 is ridiculous.

Now imagine that you are the reader and that you support Senate Bill 211.

In the first topic sentence, there's nothing here to put you on the defensive. This is only a possibility for you to consider. The writer assumes that it would be an unintended consequence, not a malicious act by its sponsors. The sentence is objective about its concern. As a supporter, this sentence is still challenging for you. You may not want to hear this. However, because the writer brings it up respectfully, you are likely to read on with open mind. The writer has earned enough credibility for that.

The second topic sentence is less precise, so you're not sure what to expect from the paragraph, but the real barrier is the word "threat." Senate Bill 211 might indeed be a threat, so the idea might be accurate, but that word suggests intentional harm, and that could make you feel defensive about the bill, even though you don't know yet what the writer means by this word. The vagueness gives the impression that the entire bill is a broad threat, too, which you know is not true. The writer has made the job of convincing you more difficult by using this inflammatory word.

The third topic sentence is simply insulting, and as a supporter, you know that the bill doesn't warrant that kind of disrespect. It's thoughtful work. It might not be perfect, but it wasn't written by baboons. When you see a vague and insulting topic sentence like that, it almost doesn't matter what follows. If you read the paragraph at all, you will read it with distrust for this writer. A single, unprofessional word has cost the writer most of his or her credibility.

Even in conversation, you can see how professionalism works when it comes to word choice. When you speak within a professional context — to a traffic court judge, for example — you know that it is in your best interest to be polite and respectful. Your careful choice of words shows the judge that you are taking this moment seriously, and that in turn helps the judge to take you seriously as you explain why exactly you were speeding past a grade school at forty-five miles per hour. On the other hand, if you jokingly ask the judge what she's wearing under that robe or use the word "turd-like" to describe your car, you demonstrate that you are not taking the moment seriously enough. Your case will not be considered as carefully.

Be Precise

Choosing the right word rarely means choosing the only possible right word. English is such a sprawling language that you have many options for capturing your meaning. Being precise means choosing not just any correct word but the word or words that explain an idea most accurately.

Suppose, for example, that you are writing an essay that will explain how the social governance systems used by one indigenous tribe in North America to restrain antisocial behavior were superior to the religious systems used by the Massachusetts Bay Colony — at the same time, and in the same general area. Your thesis statement could introduce that idea in many different ways:

> Indians were just as good as the white settlers, if not better.

> Native North Americans had governmental systems that were as effective in governing their citizens as the colonial government's systems.

> The social governance systems of the indigenous peoples of New England were more effective in curbing antisocial behavior than the religious government of the Massachusetts Bay Colony.

In all of these examples — I am happy to report — no thesis statement uses any out-and-out wrong words. There's no "wight" where we need "white" or "emigrants" when we need "immigrants." However, you can see that some sentences capture the idea more accurately than others, and this comes from using more precise words. Let's consider the first topic sentence:

> Indians were just as good as the white settlers, if not better.

The most glaringly vague word is "good," which can be used in so many ways — effective, legal, moral, ethical, attractive, and so on — that it really doesn't mean anything on its own. It should be replaced by a more precise word or phrase that captures the standard by which something is judged good. If by "good" you mean that the results are worth the cost, for example, then just say "cost-effective."

"Indians" is another big term that could be used to refer to residents of India or — disrespectfully, many would say — to indigenous peoples throughout the Americas. Does this idea apply to all of these people? I don't think so. It applies to some smaller subgroup within this gigantic category of people. So which subgroup did you study? Use the correct term for that subgroup.

"White settlers" is another overly general term that needs to be more precisely defined. It doesn't set any boundaries on time, so it includes all white settlers, from Vikings onward. The research for this paper was much narrower, so the terms should be narrower, too. Once you narrow your focus to a specific time frame, then the "white" part will need work, too, because early immigration tends to be defined by points of origin rather than ethnic makeup.

Finally, even with a more precisely stated focus on subgroups, is the paper really trying to compare entire groups of peoples? That means looking at all aspects of human life among these subgroups. There's not enough time for you to cover all of that, student writer — not in this paragraph, and not in a three-volume book series. So refining "Indians" and "white settlers" should probably be stated even more precisely to identify the much narrower point of comparison you are making — diet, care for elderly, religious training, footwear — something.

The second thesis statement is more precise than the first:

> Native North Americans had governmental systems that were as effective in governing their citizens as the colonial government's systems.

The broad terms for people in the first sentence have been replaced by the more precise terms. "Indians" has been replaced by "Native North Americans" — removing India, Central America, and South America from the idea. "White settlers" have been replaced by "colonial government," which removes Vikings and Oregon Trail pioneers from the idea. The paper is probably not trying to cover all Native Americans or all colonists, but this is a step in the right direction.

A better step forward is that "good" is gone, and in its place, the author has chosen words that come much closer to presenting the actual focus of the idea — a comparison of the effectiveness of Native American and colonial governments. We also see the author's opinion — the Native American systems were more effective than the colonial systems. The sentence could be streamlined a little to better focus on particular elements of the governance systems, but this is still a more precise sentence than the first one.

The third thesis statement is better still:

> The social governance systems of the indigenous peoples of New England were more effective in curbing antisocial behavior than the religious government of the Massachusetts Bay Colony.

It more precisely defines which Northern Native Americans and European colonists were studied, and it more clearly states the basis for judging one government to be more effective — curbing antisocial behavior.

There's some vagueness about what exactly is being studied — which tribes? which years? — but this is still a big step forward. It wouldn't be too hard to refine this a little more by replacing "the indigenous peoples of New England" with actual tribal names and adding the actual years from the evidence that was examined. With those refinements, this topic sentence will be precise enough to let us know — accurately — what details to expect from the supporting sentences of this paragraph.

Common Word-Choice Errors

For some reason, writers of English tend to make a lot of the same word-choice mistakes over and over again. Most of these are sound-based errors, part of this difficult transition from informal to formal writing. Usually the confused words sound the same but mean something different. A dictionary and your willingness to use it will help you to avoid these common errors, but it also helps to learn about the errors you are supposed to avoid.

Words That Sound the Same

With words that sound the same — homonyms — the problem is not usually that you don't know the difference between them. The problem is usually that you didn't notice that you used the wrong word. It's a problem of proofreading, in other words.

Unfortunately, your readers don't care about honest mistakes like that. Even if your reader suspects that you do know the difference between "bare" and "bear," using "bare" when you mean "bear" creates the suspicion that you don't. And it distracts readers from your ideas.

Here are some of the more frequent homonym errors to avoid:

accept/except

"Accept" is a verb that means to receive or admit something. "Except" is almost always used as a preposition that means "other than" or "excluding." With this one, it might help to remember the noun forms of these words — acceptance and exception — to remember which word to use.

> I do not *accept* your excuse. (verb)

> Everyone took the test *except* you. (preposition)

bare/bear

"Bare" is either a verb that means to empty or uncover something or an adjective that means that something has been emptied or uncovered. "Bear" is first of all a large animal that goes into a bar and orders a beer. It is also a verb that means to carry or endure something.

> A *bear* walked into a bar. (animal)

> The bartender could not *bear* to be asked for a beer. (to endure)

> He *bared* his teeth at the bear and growled. (to uncover, animal)

> "What?" said the *bear*. "Is it because I'm *bare*?" (animal, uncovered)

The phrase "bear with me" means to put up with me, to endure whatever I'm doing that might test your patience. If you write "bare with me," you are inviting people to get naked with you. If that's what you want, that's fine. I won't judge.

cite/sight/site

"Cite" is a verb that means either to mention the source of an idea or information, to quote someone, or to give you a citation for traveling forty-five miles per hour in a school zone. "Sight" is a noun that refers to vision or to something you see. "Site" is either a noun that means a place — including a place on the Internet — or a verb that means to put something in a particular place.

> You are quite a *sight* today. (vision)

> I decided to *site* my new house on that site outside of town. (location)

> When the officer *cited* me for speeding, I *cited* Mario Andretti: "If everything seems under control, then you're not going fast enough." (ticket, quotation)

complement/compliment

"Complement" — with an "e" after the "l"— is either a verb that usually means to complete something or the noun that makes something complete. A "compliment" — with an "i" after the "l" — is either a verb that means something nice you say to your mother when you can tell that she is mad at you about something, or it's a noun, the nice thing you say.

> I *complimented* my mother on her winter coat. (verb, to say a nice thing)

> It was a good *complement* to her winter hat and galoshes. (noun, a thing that matches or completes)

> She rejected my *compliment*. (noun, a nice thing that was said)

council/counsel

"Council" is a noun that means either a group of people who give direction and advice to others or the direction and advice that they give. "Counsel" is a verb that means to give council to someone.

> The *council* met on Thursday to consider my case. (noun)

> They *counseled* me to give up and go home. (verb)

> I bravely said that I would think about their *council*. (noun)

have/of

Most of the time, these words aren't misused. "Have" is used correctly as a verb, and "of" is used correctly as a preposition. Life goes on. The trouble arises when "have" is used with a verb like "should" or "would," like this:

I should've known better.

For many writers, that word sounds the same as this:

I should *of* known better.

In this situation, only "have" is correct. "Of" is always a preposition that can be used in a lot of ways but usually means "coming from" or "made of" or "belonging to."

We should *have* bought that barrel. (verb)

It was a barrel *of* monkeys. (preposition)

it's/its

This is the most common of all these mistakes. We're so used to adding "s" to a noun to make it possessive, that we yearn with all our hearts to add it to the pronoun "it." Even when we know that possessive pronouns never use apostrophes, we yearn. If I'm not paying close attention, I'll sometimes do it by accident. However, "it's" is always and only a contraction for "it is" or "it has." "Its" is the possessive form of the pronoun "it."

It's been raining all day. (contraction for "it has")

It's a double rainbow! (contraction for "it is")

Its colors are so incredibly beautiful (possessive pronoun, the colors belonging to "it")

passed/past

"Passed" is always a form of the verb "to pass," so it can refer to going past something, to dying, or to throwing a football at some point in your distant childhood. "Past" is a more flexible word that refers to distance or time in many different ways, but it is never a verb.

I *passed* the basketball to the wrong team. (to pass)

In the *past*, my coach screamed at me for that sort of thing. (time)

This time, he walked *past* the end of the bench and *passed* out. (distance, to pass)

patience/patients

"Patience" is the calm endurance that caregivers need when they care for others. "Patients" are people who are being cared for.

> The nurse was assigned ten new *patients*. (people receiving care)

> He lost his *patience* with them, however, and spent most of his shift smoking in the janitor's closet. (calm endurance, or lack thereof)

principal/principle

When I was a child, I was taught that the principal — that is, the person to whom my teachers sent me for mouthing off in class — was my "pal." He was my princi*pal*. Get it? He wasn't much of a pal, though. This was before children were precious. My pal had the legal right to spank me with a wooden paddle for mouthing off in class, a right he was not reluctant to exercise.

Anyway, "principal" is either an adjective that means "the most important," as in, "the principal reason," or a noun that means "the most important one," as in, my pal with the wooden paddle, or the amount I still owe on the loan for my 2007 Buick LeSabre.

"Principle" is a noun that means a guiding idea or value.

> The *principal* reason that I dislike principals is that they hate children.

> I am opposed to the *principle* of corporal punishment.

their/there/they're

This is another popular homonym error. There's not much excuse for it because these are common enough words, but in case you're not sure about the meaning, here you go. "Their" is the possessive form of the pronoun "they." As with all possessive pronouns, no apostrophe is used with this word. "There" is an adverb that describes where something is located. "They're" is a contraction for "they are."

> The dog is out *there* in the backyard with the kids. (adverb)

> *They're* using the dog as a horse. (contraction)

> *Their* horse is about to bite off their noses. (possessive pronoun)

to/too/two

"To" is a preposition that can be used in many different ways — literally and figuratively — but that usually means something like "toward" or "in the direction of." "Too" is an adverb that either means "also" or "more than enough." "Two" is a number. It means one more than one.

> She has *too* many cats. (adverb)
>
> She gave one cat *to* me. (preposition)
>
> I already had *two* cats. (number)
>
> Now I have *too* many cats, *too*. (adverb)

you're/your

This is cousin to there/they're/their. "You're" is a contraction for "you are," and "your" is the possessive form of the pronoun "you."

> *You're* not going to believe this. (contraction)
>
> *Your* mother just sold all *your* Little League trophies on eBay. (possessive pronoun)

weather/wether/whether

"Weather" is a word you know. It's either a noun that means it's raining outside or a verb that means you're enduring some weather — literally or figuratively. "Wether" is a noun that means a castrated sheep. I'm not joking. "Whether" is a conjunction that introduces some doubt or uncertainty about one or more possibilities. It's often used with "or not."

> The *weather* outside is frightful. (climate)
>
> The *wethers* outside also look pretty unhappy, but it's probably not because of the weather. (sheep, climate)
>
> I don't know *whether* I will go outside today. (conjunction)

who's/whose

"Who's" is always a contraction for "who is" or "who has." As a contraction, it is best for informal writing. "Whose" is the possessive form of all three relative pronouns — that, which, and who.

Who's going to pay me for mowing the lawn? (contraction for "who is")

Who's paid you for mowing the lawn in the past? (contraction for "who has")

Whose lawnmower should I use? (relative pronoun)

Other Homonym Errors to Avoid

You should also watch out for the following homonyms, and if you aren't sure about the meaning of any words in this list, care enough to open a dictionary and look up the meanings:

ad/add	heal/heel	retch/wretch
aid/aide	hear/here	right/rite/write
altar/alter	idle/idol	root/rout/route
aisle/isle	jam/jamb	seam/seem
bail/bale	lets/let's	shear/sheer
bloc/block	miner/minor	shudder/shutter
born/borne	naval/navel	sic/sick
break/brake	pair/pare/pear	steak/stake
by/bye/buy	palate/palette/pallet	sole/soul
canon/cannon/canyon	payed/paid	spade/spayed
censor/sensor	peace/piece	straight/strait
core/corps	peak/peek/pique	taught/taut
dew/do/doo/due	peal/peel	threw/through/thru
dual/duel	pedal/peddle	vain/vane/vein
fair/fare	plain/plane	vary/very
faze/phase	pole/poll	wail/wale/whale
feint/faint	pray/prey	waver/waiver
flair/flare	raise/raze/rays	which/witch
foul/fowl	rain/reign/rein	

Words That Sound Similar

Just as homonyms can cause problems for student writers, many words with different meanings sound fairly similar. If you use the wrong one, the meaning of your sentence will be messed up, and so will your credibility with careful readers. Here are some common errors to understand and avoid:

affect/effect

"Affect" is usually used as a verb that means to influence something. "Effect" is usually used as a noun that means the result of some action or influence.

> Your whining does not *affect* me. (verb)

> Your whining will have no positive *effect*. (noun)

Because this is English, there are exceptions to this usage. You can use "affect" as a noun that is short for "affectation" or, in the social sciences, as a noun that means "a display of emotion." If you are a manager or administrator, you can also use "effect" as a verb that means to create a change.

> Even when I stole his pizza, there was no change in his affect. (affect as a noun)

> Many administrators think that they can effect educational reform. (effect as a verb)

bias/biased

"Bias" is a noun that either means a diagonal line or pattern — such as when used with something woven — or prejudice. "Biased" is an adjective that means something has either type of bias.

> Coach Nelson has a *bias* in favor of the Nebraska Cornhuskers. (noun)

> Wherever the Cornhuskers are concerned, Coach Nelson is *biased*. (adjective)

choose/chose

"Choose" is a verb that means to select. "Chose" is the past tense form of that verb. I wish there were more to it than that. There's not.

> Today I *choose* to do my homework. (present tense)

> Yesterday I *chose* to do my laundry. (past tense)

coma/comma

The misuse of these two words is always embarrassing. It happens, I think, because people sometimes sound out "comma," and when you sound it out, you only need one "m." Your stupid spell checker is once again worthless in warning you, so you have to memorize the two words. "Coma" is the state of prolonged unconsciousness. "Comma" is a punctuation mark that you do not add to a sentence when you hear a pause.

> Use a *comma* to separate each item in a list of three or more items. (punctuation mark)

> If you use a *comma* whenever you hear a pause, your writing professor may slip into a *coma* when reading your paper. (punctuation mark, unconsciousness)

farther/further

These are similar words that are used to compare distances. "Farther" is only used for comparing physical distances. You can remember this because the "far" in "farther" refers to physical distances — while "fur," I suppose, refers to the hair on an animal's arms. "Further" is used for everything except for physical distances — the length of a speech, for example. It means "in addition to" or simply "more."

> You traveled *farther* today than I ever will. (physical distance)

> I was willing to bid $20 for the baseball cap, but you went *further*. (not physical distance)

> Our differences require *further* study. (not physical distance)

later/latter

"Later" is either an adjective that means I am more late than you, or it is an adverb that means something happened further down the time line. Except when it's used in the phrase "latter-day" to mean present or recent times, "latter" is a noun that means the last of two or more things that you have already mentioned.

> *Later* in the morning, I ordered a lunch of soup and crackers. (adverb)

> The *latter* were saltine crackers. (noun, the last of a set of things)

And in case you're wondering, "former" means the first of the things that you've already mentioned:

> The former was tomato soup.

loose/lose

"Loose" is either a verb that means to release something from restraint or, more commonly, an adjective that describes something that is free from restraint — physical or moral. "Lose" is a verb that means you cannot find your car keys.

> On Halloween, I *loose* the dogs on trick-or-treaters. (verb, to unleash)

> The dogs are then *loose* in the neighborhood. (adjective)

> I *lose* a lot of neighborhood friends on Halloween. (verb, to not retain)

sense/since

"Sense" is either a verb that means to perceive something or a noun that usually means one of your human faculties for perceiving something — sight, hearing, touch, and so on. "Since" is a much more flexible word that can be used as an adverb, preposition, or conjunction to mean "from then until now." It can also be used as a subordinating conjunction to mean "because."

> I *sense* your frustration. (verb, to perceive)

> I am mostly using my *sense* of hearing, but I can also *sense* your fists punching me in the arm. (noun, verb, to perceive)

> You have been frustrated *since* Tuesday. (preposition, from then until now)

> *Since* you're so frustrated, I will probably leave now. (subordinating conjunction, because)

than/then

"Than" is always used to make comparisons, and it's often used with a companion word like "rather," "more," or "less." "Then" is an adverb that usually means "at that time" or "next in order." It can also be used with "if" to introduce a consequence.

> As children, Nadine received more allowance *than* me. (comparison)

> My mother didn't think I needed allowance back *then*. (adverb, at that time)

> If wishes were fishes, my mother used to say, *then* we'd all be pretty sick of fish. (introduces consequence, comparison)

were/we're/where

Depending on your pronunciation, all of these words may be homonyms, but in most cases, at least one is pronounced differently. No matter how you pronounce them, however, they all mean something different, so you have to be careful choosing which spelling to use. "Were" is a past tense form of the verb "to be." "We're" is a contraction for "we are." "Where" is an adverb or conjunction that means "at a particular place." It's often used with questions.

> Where are you going? (adverb)
>
> We're going to the beach. (contraction, we are)
>
> You were at the beach yesterday. (verb)
>
> We go where we go. (conjunction)

Other Similar-Sounding Errors to Avoid

You should also watch out for the following sets of words that sound the same and mean something different. If you see words you aren't sure about, open a dictionary and look up their meanings:

advice/advise	ensure/insure
clench/clinch	envelop/envelope
conscience/conscious	incite/insight
decent/descent/dissent	moral/morale
desert/dessert	mute/moot
emigrate/immigrate	precede/proceed
elicit/illicit	set/sit
entomology/etymology	

Words for Nerds

Finally, there are some sets of words whose correct use depends on a more precise understanding of how the words should be used in formal writing. You can usually get away with using either word in conversation because no one but English nerds will correct you — and let's be honest, who cares what they think? However, in formal writing, using these words correctly shows your professional reader that you are more educated and skillful with language than the average person. It gives you credibility. It helps you to be taken more seriously.

These distinctions are more complicated than just a matter of definition. In most cases, the definitions are similar, so you have to know which word to use in a particular situation. So this will take a little longer than the previous sections. But just think of the rewards — soon you can be snooty with all the people who aren't as well educated as you.

among/amongst/between

There's a rule of thumb out there that you use "between" with two items and "among" with more than two items. Like so many of the rules of thumb we've discussed, this rule of thumb is also bogus. It will work sometimes and fail sometimes because it focuses on the wrong thing — numbers. The real thing to look at is whether the items are distinctly identified. If each item is identified, you use "between," even if there are more than two items:

> The debate about beets *between* my mother, my sister, and myself quickly turned ugly. (three distinct items)

> To avoid the conflict in the dining room, the cats hid *between* the toilet and the bathtub. (two distinct items)

You use "among" when you are talking about things that are not as clearly defined, even if there is only one thing that is made of many parts:

> I always feel lonely among my family members.

> In fact, I feel lonely among all my family and my friends.

> I am only truly myself among my cats.

This distinct versus indistinct factor also applies when you use it with places. If you are talking about traveling from one distinct place to another, use "between":

> I walked between my apartment and the grocery store.

If you are talking about indistinct places, use "among":

> At the grocery store, I wandered among the aisles.

Finally, "amongst" is still out there as an old-fashioned variation of "among." If you live in Great Britain or the eighteenth century, then you can use "amongst," where it is slightly more common. Otherwise, use "among."

fewer/less

These words both mean "not as much," as in, "less love" and "fewer kisses." The trick is to use each with the correct type of noun. You use "fewer" with nouns that can be counted:

> I have fewer friends than my sister.

> There are fewer birds in the sky every time I walk by.

You will not be terribly surprised to learn that these nouns are called **count nouns**. There's another technical term for you. You know that nouns are count nouns if you can change them from singular nouns into plural nouns, like "friend" to "friends" and "bird" to "birds."

Many nouns cannot be counted, even though they consist of more than one thing. These are called **mass nouns**. For example, the word "garbage" usually refers to a lot of undesirable things, but you refer to it as a single unit — a mass. These nouns cannot be changed from singular to plural. You just have "garbage." You do not have "garbages." For mass nouns, you use "less" because there is less of that mass:

> Put less of your garbage in my garage.

To confuse you further, be aware that some nouns can be used as *either* count *or* mass nouns. The noun "salt," for example, is mostly used as a mass noun that refers to many grains of a particular substance:

> Please put less salt on my french fries.

And not:

> Please put less salts on my french fries.

However, you can still use the word "salts." It's a count noun when you are talking about more than one type of salt, and types can be counted:

> Because of my recent pay cut, I will buy fewer bath salts this year.

good/well

These words both mean the same thing — not bad — but they are used to describe different types of words. "Good" is an adjective, so it describes nouns:

> You are a good player.

> The baby was a good little crier.

"Well" is an adverb, so it describes verbs:

> You played well today.

> The baby sitting behind me on the plane cried well and for hours.

In conversation, you can get away with using "good" for nouns or verbs. If someone asks you how you're doing, you can say, "Good." Only snooty people like my former girlfriend will think that you are ignorant for not saying, "I am well. And you, my good fellow?" However, with formal writing and with people like Denise, the standards are higher, so you should use "well" when you are writing about a verb.

There's one slight wrinkle, though. "Well" can also be used with a verb to create an adjective phrase that describes a noun:

> That was a well-played game.

> Her sins are well documented.

If the adjective phrase comes before the noun, then you hyphenate the words to show that they work together to create one meaning. If the adjective phrase comes after the noun as part of the predicate, then you don't hyphenate. I'm not sure why you don't, but you don't.

who/whom

There is a lot of confusion about which of these words to use and when. There's a good reason for that confusion, too — it's confusing. It requires an understanding of English grammar that few dare obtain. Fortunately, there's a short cut, and although we've been warned all our lives about how bad short cuts are, we're going to take it.

We'll start with a quick definition. Both of these words are **relative pronouns** that refer to persons. You can use them to ask a question about a person:

Who threw my cat?

Or you can use them to create a relative clause about a person:

The boy *who threw your cat* is named Jojo.

The choice about which relative pronoun to use depends on the type of noun phrase you are asking about or referring to. If it's a subject noun phrase, you use "who." If it's some other kind of noun phrase, you use "whom."

So consider this bit of information:

Jojo threw my cats to his brother.

Now look at how I use "who" and "whom" to refer to the three different noun phrases in this sentence:

Sentence	Explanation
I don't care much for Jojo, *who* threw my cats to his brother.	Use "who" because it refers to the subject of the original sentence — Jojo — and he is a person.
However, I do like my cats, *whom* Jojo threw to his brother.	Use "whom" because it refers to my cats, who are not the subject of the original sentence and who are people, too, kind of.
To *whom* did Jojo throw the cats?	Use "whom" because it because it refers to Jojo's brother, who is not the subject of the original sentence and who is a person.

You see how that works? I use "who" when I refer to the subject of the original sentence. I use "whom" for the other noun phrases. And I only use "who" or "whom" because these are people, not objects. If they were objects, I would have to use "which" or "that."

Even before you have a firm, grammatical grasp of subjects and other types of noun phrases, you can use your informal use of regular pronouns to figure out which relative pronoun to use. Let's go back to this horrifying cat experience:

> Jojo threw my cats to his brother.

If you replace the noun phrase "Jojo" with a pronoun, you would write:

> *He* threw my cats to his brother.

Because Jojo is the subject of the original sentence, the one who does the throwing, and "he" is the subject form of the pronoun for individual males. But if you replace "his brother," it's a different story. You'd write :

> Jojo threw my cats to *him.*

Because Jojo's brother is *not* the subject of the original sentence.

And that's the short cut for "who" and "whom." If you'd replace a noun phrase with the regular pronouns "him" or "them" or "her" or "us," then you use the relative pronoun "whom" in a relative clause. Similarly, if you could answer a question with the regular pronouns "him" or "them" or "her" or "us," you use "whom" in the question. Otherwise, you use "who." So:

> *Who* threw my cats? He did. I don't like Jojo, *who threw my cats to his brother.*

> To *whom* did Jojo throw my cats? To him. I also don't think much of Jojo's brother, *to whom Jojo threw my cats.*

> *Whom* did Jojo throw to his brother? Them. But I love my poor cats, *whom Jojo threw to his brother.*

One last thing, and then we're done. Do you notice that little "to" before the "whom" in the second example above? When the noun phrase you're referring to follows a preposition — like "to," for example — that preposition travels with the relative pronoun. So you should say this:

> *To whom* did Jojo throw my cats?

And not this:

Whom did Jojo throw my cats *to?*

That's not a huge thing, but as long as you're trying to use "whom" correctly, you might as well do this correctly, too.

Now you can see why people who understand how to use "who" and "whom" correctly make such a big deal about it. They've had to work hard to get there.

Other Tricky Word Sets and Further Nerd-Making

This level of word distinction won't make or break you as a formal writer, and especially when you are just learning to write college essays. However, the more you work on these finer points, the more polished your writing becomes, and that makes your writing even more effective.

Here are some additional sets of words that require a closer examination:

beside/besides	done/finished
blond/blonde	i.e./e.g.
compose/comprise	lie/lay
disinterested/uninterested	like/as
can/may	may/might
Chicano/Latino/Hispanic	people/persons

Whether or not you get nerdy about it, though, you should own a good dictionary to help you with spelling and choosing the right word for your ideas. A little paperback dictionary is okay for spelling help, but to get into the details, start with a collegiate dictionary like *Merriam-Webster's Collegiate Dictionary* or *Webster's New World College Dictionary* — or any other dictionary with "college" in the title. This will give you more detailed definitions and some notes on using similar words correctly.

Once you get in the habit of looking up the meaning of words, you'll gradually find yourself enjoying the practice. I know, you may doubt that, but it really will happen. You'll enjoy being able to use words with more confidence, and you'll find some amusement in listening to other people make the same mistakes that you no longer make.

The Big Ideas

This chapter introduced you to some important ideas about word choice with formal writing. There's a lot to think about, but the main thing is to simply slow down and pay attention to your words — and use a good dictionary whenever you're not sure about something.

Here are the big ideas from this chapter:

1. Choose the right word: Many words sound like other words. Make sure that the word you use has the meaning you intend. If you're not sure which word is the right one, take one minute from your busy schedule and look them both up in a dictionary.

2. Spell your words correctly: Use a dictionary and your own good sense. Don't trust spell checkers because spell checkers are stupid.

3. Be professional: Use words that are appropriate for a professional settings. Do not distract from your ideas or offend your readers with rudeness or too much informality.

4. Be precise: English is a sprawling language that offers many words that have similar meanings. Being precise means choosing not just any correct word but the word or words that explain an idea most accurately.

5. Study and avoid common errors: Writers of English tend to make a lot of the same word-choice mistakes over and over again. If you study those common errors, you are more likely to avoid them.

The College Essay Is Something You Do

Part Two Overview

The Writing of Formal Writing

The first half of this book presented the *form* of formal writing. It showed you the expectations for formal papers, and you can see that those expectations are higher than they were with the informal papers of your misspent youth. Meeting those expectations will take some work, and that's fine. You're ready to be taken seriously.

But it's important to remember that formal writing is just a delivery system for ideas — for *your* ideas — so while yes, you need to follow the rules of formal writing to be taken seriously, it's your ideas that matter more. They are what make your formal papers different from the other papers that your professor reads. More importantly, they are the best reward for writing the paper in the first place.

This emphasis on ideas means that you need a writing process that focuses on developing great ideas. You can't just sit at the computer and see what your brain comes up with. No offense to your brain, but it can only do so much on its own. You have to help your brain with a writing process that feeds it new information and helps it build better ideas. And thankfully, that's just the sort of writing process that the second half of this book presents:

1. **Educate yourself about your topic.** Get to know your topic and then narrow your focus to dig deeper into the information about one small part of your topic.

2. **Identify and improve one good idea of your own about the topic.** State your idea clearly in a single sentence and then improve your idea by making that sentence more precise and accurate.

3. **Carefully present your idea.** Plan your essay, draft it, and then revise and proofread it.

This process varies a bit with different types of college writing, but the same basic pattern persists. You begin in relative ignorance, you work hard to enlighten yourself, and then you present one enlightening idea to others. And that, student writer, is what makes formal writing so much more satisfying than informal writing — those enlightening ideas. Papers will come and go. Grades will rise and fall. But the ideas stay with you.

This kind of satisfaction doesn't happen with the first paper, of course. It takes time to get comfortable with the rules of formal writing, and it takes time to learn how to educate yourself and develop better ideas. The early rewards for your efforts are likely to be a lot of frustration. But so what? What new skill *isn't* frustrating at first? Welding? Ballet? Marriage? Lawn bowling? Anything complicated is frustrating at first, and almost everything worth learning is complicated. That's just how life works.

When I was nine years old, my mother gave me the option of not taking piano lessons anymore. "Darn it, Roy," she said. "I have had it up to *here* with your complaining. Go or don't go. I don't give a hoot." So, of course, freed from the dread of my mother's hooting, I quickly ended my year and five months of piano lessons. Because piano lessons were *so boring*. Hours upon hours of practice, and for what? My only reward was a painful, hesitating version of "Twinkle, Twinkle, Little Star" that made everyone at the Spring Into Music recital grit their teeth.

My sister Nadine, on the other hand, stayed with her piano lessons for *thirteen years*, and now she can sit down at a piano, close her eyes, and just play whatever comes to mind — any of a thousand songs. It's a beautiful thing. It makes her almost tolerable. And when she's done, she opens her eyes, smiles that pinched little smile of hers, and says, "Your turn, Roy."

Don't let that be your story, student writer.

Learn how to educate yourself and write formal papers with the foresight and dedication I lacked at age nine. Study this writing process, and put it to good use. Yes, it may be a little frustrating at first, but the frustration will be worth it. Be patient. Keep writing. Ask for help. It won't be long before you break through the frustration and begin to truly enjoy thinking for yourself and sharing your ideas with others.

Chapter 6
The College Essay Means Thinking for Yourself

Just as the formal papers described in the first half of this book are different from informal papers, the writing process for formal papers is also different from what you used to do to create informal papers. It's one thing — and a good thing, by the way — to understand what formal writing *is*. It's another and more important thing to understand what formal writing requires you to *do*. If you try to create a formal paper with informal methods, you will be frustrated by the papers you create and the grades they receive. It will feel like a waste of time, and in fact, it will be.

In this chapter, we'll start by looking at what *not* to do — those old, insufficient strategies that keep you from thinking for yourself. Then we'll move on to a brief introduction of a three-step writing process that will help you write effective formal papers and live a more satisfying life.

How Not to Write: Youthful Rituals

Whenever I ask a new class of writing students to explain their process for writing essays, the answers as always the same. Most respond with a striking combination of ignorance and confidence. For these writers, the writing process is essentially a mystery, but it's a mystery that they have conquered with various rituals. Here's one typical explanation:

> Whenever I have to write an essay, I sit in my room and turn off all the lights except for the computer monitor, which goes to a screen saver of traveling through the universe, like on *Star Trek*. I light a candle to help me relax. Vanilla is good. After that, I wait for an idea to come to me. Usually something comes to me within five minutes. I never question what it is. I

> just go with it. I write until I get it all out and onto paper — or the computer, actually. Then I stop. If there's time, I come back later to check spelling and stuff, but I almost never change anything.

Good luck with not changing anything, student writer.

A second common method is just as magical, but it's less overtly so. This process relies on the subconscious mind:

> When I need to write an essay, the first thing I do is get online and just read about whatever the topic is for like an hour. Sometimes I take longer, but only if I'm into it. Then I just write about whatever I've read. The information all kind of flows together onto the page. I go over it once to smooth things out, but if I spend more time than that, the process starts to break down.

The process starts to break down, semiconscious student writer, because it's not a process. You're relying on your subconscious mind to piece together whatever information is floating around in your brain. When you spend more time on it, you realize that you have no idea what you're doing.

A third approach depends less on magic or the subconscious mind and more on other people. This isn't plagiarism because the students aren't passing off someone else's ideas as their own, but it does rely on something other than the student writer's ability to think. Here's an example:

> Whenever I have a paper assignment, my mother and I sit down and talk things through, and she lets me know when I have something that seems like it would be a good paper. Then I go off and write it on my own. That might take an hour. Then we work on revising it together. She was a teacher for many years, so she knows about how to write papers. She's the one who taught me that an essay should have three supporting paragraphs, which I still think is the best way to do it. None of my previous teachers have had any problems with it. In fact, I have always gotten excellent grades in all my English classes UNTIL THIS TERM. I used to enjoy writing — A LOT.

Sorry for ruining your life, student writer! It happens.

What you see in all the examples is an abdication of the writers' responsibility to think for themselves. Instead, they let their moms or their subconscious minds or mysterious forces of the universe do the writing for them, as if the writing process is more than they can handle on their own.

However, writing the college essay is just one more set of actions that can be learned and improved upon. No magic is required. Mothers are entirely optional. Learning this process might feel awkward at first, but for humans, awkward is normal. Awkward is a sign that you're getting somewhere. You've done this a hundred times before with a hundred other new skills. It's not like you left the womb knowing how to tie your shoes or drive a car or find a moderately priced Thai restaurant.

> **"Writing the college essay is just a set of actions that can be learned and improved upon. No magic is required. Mothers are entirely optional."**

Another problem might be that at some dark moment in your past, a teacher actually told you that you were just a bad writer. If you took that teacher seriously, you might be clinging even more desperately to whatever rituals seem to work. But here's the real story with an incident like that — your teacher was just a bad teacher. You might not have had the skills you needed to be an effective writer *at the time*, but your teacher was blaming you for his or her failure to teach you how to improve. What a rotten teacher! I'm sorry for your terrible luck. However, that doesn't give you a pass. You need to forgive that lousy teacher, set down your rituals, and get back to work.

People may naturally be more or less comfortable in their ability to use written language, but everyone can learn how to write the college essay. All you have to do is start out simply and get better with practice. You might not become a professional writer, but with enough practice, you *can* become competent and comfortable and able to use a more thoughtful writing process.

How Also Not to Write — The Knucklehead

A fourth inadequate process is also fairly common, particularly among informal writers who have a way with words. For them, it's the hardest bad habit to leave behind because it's worked so well for so long. Here's one student's explanation:

> The way I write a paper is to figure out what I want to say and then look for information that will support it. I usually know what I want to say right away. Ideas just come to me like that. I'm not opinionated, but I have a lot of good ideas. If I can find enough stuff to support my idea, then I just start writing and put it all in the paper. If I can't find enough information, then either I start over with a different idea (hardly ever) or I use common knowledge to explain what I mean.

This process reminds me of waiting for my first swimming lesson to begin — hanging out in the wading pool with the other Pollywogs. I was intensely afraid of drowning in the big pool, so to convince my mother that I didn't need swimming lessons, I laid on my belly in the wading pool and flopped around. "Mom!" I yelled. "Look! I can swim! I don't need lessons!" My mother looked up from her magazine. "That ain't swimming, Roy," she said. "That's just being a knucklehead." The other mothers laughed. I felt like an idiot, but she did have a point.

It's the same point I make to students when they use the knucklehead process for writing the college essay. That ain't the college essay, student writer. That's just being a knucklehead. Yes, that thing you turned in *looks* like a college essay — you've got your own main idea, and you've found information to back it up — but it's not a college essay because you've reversed the two central steps of the writing process.

The knucklehead writing process looks like this:

1. Decide on an idea. It's probably a hunch because you don't know much about your topic, but it might also be some idea you found quickly on the Internet or that Uncle Larry told you when you were forced to visit him last summer.

2. Examine the topic for information to back up that idea — and ignore any contradictory information or ideas.

3. Present the idea and the information that supports it.

You see how that's different? Knuckleheads come up with an idea first and only then look for evidence — and only to back up their idea. Do you know where that idea came from? It came from the pile of ideas that were already sitting there in their knuckle-like heads, not from all the new ideas and information they could have studied.

This is the writing process of conspiracy theorists. They start with a suspicion: The mob assassinated President John F. Kennedy. The 9/11 attacks were an inside job. Barack Obama was born in Kenya. Paul McCartney died in 1966. Then they use that idea to judge whether information is credible or not. If a piece of information supports their idea, they say it's credible information. If anything refutes their idea, they say it's just part of the conspiracy and quickly reject it. Knuckleheads then use the information they accept to demonstrate to themselves and others that their suspicion is a really good idea — just look at how much evidence supports it!

It's possible, of course, that a suspicion is also true, so it's possible that a knucklehead's idea could become the main idea of a pretty good essay. However, that will only be an accidental outcome. Knuckleheads won't actually know whether their suspicions are good ideas because they won't have tested those ideas with a humble and honest look at the information. Instead, they'll have tested the information proudly and dishonestly with their existing suspicions. The idea they started with — good or bad — only becomes a more strongly held prejudice.

Thinking for yourself means being thoughtful about all of your ideas — no matter where they come from. It means educating yourself about a topic and then using that information to find the best available ideas. It means testing your ideas to make sure they're worthy of acceptance.

How to Write the College Essay

Learning how to write the college essay may not be a lot of fun at first. It's hard work, and hard work tends to be frustrating more than rewarding until you get the hang of it. I hated swim lessons — and not just that first summer, either, but for the next two summers until I finally graduated from Pollywogs by swimming the width of the pool, no small feat. It might be that kind of a struggle for you.

Or you might be like my sister Nadine, who passed Pollywogs on her first attempt. You might have a strong aptitude for using words. You might have had a high school teacher who expected you to think for yourself and use information to form and test your ideas. Don't worry about how quickly you succeed with this process. The point is to push ahead, whether or not it comes easily. With practice you get better, and all we care about is getting better.

Here's how the college writing process breaks down into the three main steps that were mentioned at the start of this chapter. I'll use a hard-hitting local news story to briefly illustrate how the process works. Then we'll look more closely at each step in the chapters that follow.

Step 1: Educate Yourself About Your Topic

In college, the reason you're assigned essays is so that you will have to deal firsthand with new topics and, in this way, educate yourself well enough about that new topic that you can then write a thoughtful essay. The essay is actually a byproduct of the more important self-education that's required. That's why you so rarely get to write about yourself or topics you already understand and care about. Whether you intended it or not, you're paying your professors to give you *new* topics to understand and care about. Whining to be allowed to please, please write about something you already care about will get you nowhere. That's not how this works.

The first step toward writing a good essay, then, is to embrace whatever topic has been assigned and then begin to educate yourself about that topic — whatever the topic might be. You don't have to fall in love with a topic. You just have to accept the work at hand for what it is. This is more of an arranged marriage. Love will come later. Get to know your topic with general sources of information — reference books, textbooks, talking to your professor, visiting credible websites. As you become more educated about that topic, you will start to notice surprising or odd or challenging bits of information that spark your interest or make you uncomfortable.

The second thing to do is to narrow your focus to one of these more engaging points and dig deeper into the topic with more professional and scholarly sources of information. They will give you more detailed and reliable information. Your closer examination of information will lead to your own conclusions about what that information means, and one of those conclusions can then be used as the main idea of your essay.

Early in the term, I tell students to find an article from a local newspaper and develop an essay in response. Suppose, for example, that the city council has voted to impose a fifty dollar tax on citizens who raise chickens within the city limits. Those hipster, urban chicken owners don't like the tax, but the city council says the tax is needed to pay for someone to oversee chicken raising operations. The only alternative would be to ban chickens entirely.

> **"As you get to know your topic, you might quickly develop an opinion of your own.... Treat that opinion like the annoying cousin who's been sleeping on your couch for the last three weeks and shows no signs of leaving. Don't encourage it."**

With a topic like this, you might start the writing process by getting to know the issue through the newspaper article. That gives you the basic information. And any kind of tax is sure to generate debate, so you can use the newspaper to find those complaints in the letters-to-the-editor section. What do the chicken owners have to say? Is anyone in favor of this tax — or opposed to chickens?

As you get to know your topic, you might quickly develop an opinion of your own. If so, don't be a knucklehead about it. Treat that opinion like the annoying cousin who's been sleeping on your couch for the last three weeks and shows no signs of leaving. Don't encourage it. In fact, challenge it whenever possible. You need to keep an open mind at this point, and that means testing any hunches about your topic rather skeptically. A hunch tends to limit your focus to information that's relevant to that idea, and you need to consider all the information you can find so that your idea will be as thoughtful as possible.

To dig deeper into the topic of raising chickens within city limits, you can do three things — the same three options you'll have with any topic. First, you can deal with the topic firsthand. Talk to the chicken owners. Talk to the chicken haters. Talk to the chickens. If you're a shy person, you might read what these people have said by reading a transcript of the city council meeting to get the exact words of everyone.

Your second option is to see what the experts have to say. With most topics, experts have been there before you and have written down their own conclusions about a topic. Just go to your college library and find what the experts have written. And trust me, there are experts writing about *every* topic.

Your third option is talk to people who can help you find the information you need. Talk to your professor. Talk to the reference librarians in your campus library. You might know someone whose job is related to your topic — the retired chicken inspector who moved into the apartment downstairs, for example. She seems nice enough.

> "Welcome to the rest of your life, unsuspecting student writer! The only thing you'll need to do from now until the grave is educate yourself about one new topic after another."

Once you start exploring a topic, you will be shocked and amazed to see the complexity of your topic expand outward in a dozen directions. That brings you to the second phase of self-education — narrowing your focus to examine one smaller and engaging aspect of your topic. By narrowing your focus, you're able to invest more time in a smaller range of information — to do more with less. This allows you to become a mini-expert on that subtopic, and that's what you need to be in order to write about it.

Many student writers aren't happy about this kind of commitment to an assigned topic. They think they have more important things to do than educate themselves. To them, I say welcome to the rest of your life, unsuspecting student writer! The only thing you'll need to do from now until the grave is educate yourself about one new topic after another. It's not just college, either. Life itself will assign you all sorts of unexpected and unwanted topics. It will often be fun work, but even when it's not any fun, the alternative — letting other people do your thinking for you — is far worse.

We'll look more closely at how to educate yourself in chapter 7.

Step 2: Identify and Improve Your Main Idea

At some point, even with a topic as straightforward as urban chickens — and even if you narrow your focus to some smaller subtopic, such as the rich, emotional bond between chickens and owners — you will run out of time for educating yourself about your topic. When that happens, you have to decide which of your ideas to write about. Your decision should be based on a few things — the assignment, your interest in the idea, and your honesty.

You need to show proper respect for the assignment by living within its boundaries. If you end up with an idea you love that's outside those boundaries, then at least talk to your professor about getting a waiver to make sure your idea will be acceptable. Your professor will probably go along with your plan, and if he or she doesn't, then at least you won't have wasted your time writing a paper that would probably fail to do what was expected of it.

As much as possible, keep yourself amused and engaged in the process, too. You do that by writing about an idea that *you* find engaging. If you have taken the time to educate yourself about your topic, you should have several to choose from. Pick one that comes with interesting information that you can share with readers. It's more rewarding to work with one of your own ideas than it is to write about some quick, knuckleheaded idea that you didn't discover yourself. Your readers will find it more engaging, too.

The honesty part of the equation comes from letting the information you have found guide you toward the best idea available. People usually focus on parts of a topic that are debatable or controversial. With chickens, you might not be personally invested in an idea. However, if you're writing about something that matters to you, and if the information pulls you toward an idea you didn't expect and don't like, honesty can be a challenge. Be honest anyway. Don't be a knucklehead. Make sure that your idea is accurately founded on real-world information and reasonable thinking.

Your idea needs to be precise, too. Until you define your idea precisely, you've only *kind of* decided what you think. That's not good enough. A vague idea is just a hazy cluster of potential ideas and will often lead to a reflection paper rather than an essay. To define an idea precisely, you need to translate the idea into actual words and then tinker with those words until they define your idea exactly and accurately. Regarding chickens, you might end up with a thesis statement like this:

> All chickens should be banned from within the city limits because they make noise outside of the normal hours for quiet and because most people find their smell offensive.

You could do worse than that. This sentence states your opinion and supplies two reasons. That's pretty good. Writing your thesis statement becomes a sort of pivot point for you. Your self-education brings you to this thesis statement, and the same thesis statement becomes your starting point for Step 3 in the writing process.

We'll take a closer look at Step 2 — including a few tricks to make the process more effective — in chapter 8.

Step 3: Carefully Present Your Idea

Now it's time to share your thinking with others by presenting this new opinion of yours as the main idea of an essay. This step in the process typically breaks down into three stages: planning, drafting, and revising.

Planning: To effectively explain a complex main idea, your essay needs to lay out your thinking in detail and present readers with plenty of information. To make sure that happens, you must carefully plan your body paragraphs — figuring out what your supporting ideas will be and how they will be broken out into the actual paragraphs. Using the thesis statement from Step 2 as an example, you see that you have a least three things to talk about:

1. Chickens should be banned from within the city limits.

2. Reason: They make noise outside of the normal quiet hours.

3. Reason: Most people find their smell offensive.

If this were to be a five-paragraph trainer-essay, your planning would be done. But you're not going to go there, student writer. The five-paragraph trainer-essay is dead to you. You're writing college essays now, so you need to get into more detail, and that means looking at the evidence you gathered and figuring out how much of it you will need to use to explain your thinking.

Idea 1 for the above list — ban the chicken! — is the biggest idea to explain, so you may need to divide your evidence into several paragraphs:

1. The chicken situation — who's raising them and where

2. The chicken ban — what you mean by the ban

3. Enforcement — how you would make sure the ban was obeyed

4. Effects — how the ban would make things better

If you follow that with your two reasons for the ban, that leaves you with these six supporting ideas for the body of your essay:

1. The chicken situation — who's raising them and where

2. The chicken ban — what you mean by the ban

3. Enforcement — how you would make sure the ban was obeyed

4. Effects — how the ban would make things better

5. Reason: They make noise outside of the normal quiet hours.

6. Reason: Most people find their smell offensive.

That looks promising.

Now it's time to organize these paragraphs. The more clearly you organize your information into meaningful patterns, the more likely it is that your readers will see how all those details work together to explain your main idea. When someone throws a lot of disorganized information at you, you become confused. You don't see what all the information adds up to — if anything — and you gradually stop paying attention. You don't want to do that to your readers. It's mean.

So how might you organize these paragraphs into a pattern? You have plenty of options, as you saw back in chapter 2. For this focus, you could try a problem-and-solution pattern:

1. Problem: Chickens in town

   a. The chicken situation — who's raising them and where

   b. Problem: They make noise outside of the normal quiet hours.

   c. Problem: Most people find their smell offensive.

2. Solution: The chicken ban

   a. What you mean by the ban

   b. Enforcement — how you would make sure the ban was obeyed.

   c. Results: How the ban would make things better.

That makes sense. And really, that's all that matters, that the parts add up to a whole — make sense — in the minds of your readers. Any pattern of organization will do that.

We'll talk more about organizing your essay in chapter 9.

Drafting: This is where you put onto paper the actual words that will transfer an idea from your brain into the brains of your readers. Some writers can draft entire essays in their heads and then type them out as final drafts. These writers are so rare, however, that the federal government pays scientists to study them. I'm serious. If nobody's studying you, then you are probably not one of these writers, so plan on writing more than one draft.

It's a good idea to start by drafting the body of your essay. Student writers often get hung up on achieving the perfect opening paragraph. However, to write the perfect opening paragraph, or even an okay opening paragraph, you need to know what's in the body of the essay. So write a full paragraph for each point in your paragraph outline. If you have to expand more important or complex points into multiple paragraphs, then do so. You're the boss of that outline. Once the body is done, drafting a good opening and closing is much easier.

Drafting often leads you to unexpected discoveries about your topic or your main idea. Drafting relies on the subconscious mind to gather up the right words, and the subconscious mind, once activated, is creative and unpredictable — kind of like a four-year-old. You might discover a new wrinkle in the information, and that might lead you to an even better main idea. You might also see that a big chunk of information in your essay isn't actually relevant to your particular idea. You might have to dump it. If drafting shows you that you have to make changes, then make changes. Don't fall too deeply in love with what you've written. It's the idea that matters most, so go with the best idea.

There's more to drafting that just putting your own words together. With formal writing, you must share the information you gathered to explain yourself. Doing this honestly and accurately requires you to carefully show your readers which ideas or words are yours and which come from others. You have to give credit to those others, too, and usually by following pretty stringent, formal guidelines. Using the ideas and information of others without giving them credit is called plagiarism. That's one of the high sins of formal writing, and it's also unprofessional, so there won't be any of that.

We'll talk more about drafting in chapter 10, and we'll look at how to handle outside information in chapter 11.

Revising: This word can be used to describe any point in your writing process when you stop to look at what you're doing and try to do a better job of it. Revising in its broadest sense means "re-seeing," so that can apply to stepping back and re-seeing your thesis statement, your planned organization, your drafting — *anything*. I have no quarrel with that broad use of the word, but for our purposes, revision is mostly a matter of stepping back from your draft to polish it up so that your audience won't be distracted from your ideas.

So you might revise by introducing your chicken ban idea with a more colorful opening. You might add or subtract bits of information within the body paragraphs to more effectively explain your supporting idea about how much chickens stink. You might remove that paragraph about your ingrown toenail as a fairly distracting metaphor for chicken raising. You might find that one paragraph has so many supporting sentences that you divide it into so subsets of support.

Revision includes working on the sentences of the essay, but save most of that until after you are confident of your paragraphs. You don't want to spend time worrying about how to spell "defecation" or where to put a comma when the entire paragraph needs to be plucked from the essay like an illegal chicken — or like the feathers of an illegal chicken, I suppose. I may need to revise that illustration, in fact. My point, though, is that you shouldn't spend lots of time polishing up the punctuation in sentences that may need to be deleted. When you invest a lot of time in polishing garbage, the garbage starts to look pretty good. But it's still garbage. Make sure the sentences are helping to present your idea first. Then polish them.

Feedback is an important part of revision. Because your essay is trying to move from your brain and into the brain of another human, it helps to try out the essay on other humans, such as your professor, an editing group, a smart friend, and so on.

Student writers sometimes find it difficult to open up to feedback. They think that criticism of something they've written is criticism of their intelligence. But it's not like that. What you've written is just that — something you've written. It's not you. It's not your intelligence. It's just an essay, a tiny artifact of where you are right now as a writer. And even if it is pretty good, it's not as good as your essays will be with more practice. Once you understand that your essay is just this thing you did, like the plastic ice scraper you made in eighth-grade shop class — which by the way was a pretty decent ice scraper — it becomes a lot easier to accept and benefit from the feedback of others.

We'll look more closely at revision and proofreading in chapter 12.

How to Make the Process Work for You

In the end, and in seeming contradiction to the start of this chapter, you *will* have to discover a writing process that works specifically for you. This is the work of your brain, after all, and no two brains are alike. Brains, in this regard, are like snowflakes.

However, you do have to work within the three-step process of educating yourself about your topic, identifying and improving one main idea about that topic, and presenting your idea to others. This is how formal writing works. It's been working this way for thousands of years, and there's no reason to think that will change in your lifetime. As you get comfortable with this process, however, you should adapt and refine it so that it works best for your particular situation and habits.

You might find that the hardest step for you is narrowing your focus to one small part of your topic, and that talking to your friends — regardless of how little they actually know about your topic — is a great help. So be it. Good for you. I'm always happy to see that other people have friends. Adapt the process to include them if that's what it takes to get you moving forward.

You might find that having your own special writing place is important, or that noise is a factor. You might need complete silence. You might need music that sounds like someone being killed by an electric guitar. You might need to turn off the television. You might need to boldly reclaim those vanilla-scented candles if they really do help. It's good to figure these things out. Respect those discoveries and revise your writing process to include those conditions and precautions — but only if they don't get in the way of you thinking for yourself. Use them, but use them within the three-step writing process and not in place of it.

If you try to use this three-step writing process and it doesn't go anywhere at first, don't panic. Above all, don't go back to any inadequate processes from the past. Instead, talk to your writing professor. Most writing professors collect tricks for jump-starting writers at various stages of the writing process. It's a hobby they picked up in graduate school.

And if you don't have a writing professor, no worries. You can always search the Internet with this key phrase: "the writing process." A lot of what you find will be junk — it's the Internet, after all, where any idiot can put up a website — but you might also find just the right trick to get you going.

The Big Ideas

This chapter provided you with an overview of the process for writing formal papers. Here are the big ideas from this chapter:

1. What not to do: Do not give control of your paper to others, including mystical forces of the universe. You have to be responsible for your own ideas.

2. What also not to do: Don't be a knucklehead. Don't start with an idea and then look for evidence to back it up. Even though your final paper will *look* like an actual essay, you will not have learned anything, and you won't know if your idea is actually worth taking up space in your or your readers' brains. Instead, educate yourself and then make up your own mind about what makes sense.

3. What to do: A successful college writing process consists of three important steps:

1. Educate yourself about the topic.

2. Find and improve your main idea.

3. Present your idea carefully — by planning your essay, drafting it, and then revising it before you share it with others.

Chapter 7
Educate Yourself About Your Topic

Many student writers treat a writing assignment like it's a mild cold, something to get over as quickly as possible so that it won't interfere with any weekend plans. As soon as they receive an assignment, they put it off for the last possible moment and then — when it can't be put off a moment longer — they jump to the first obvious idea that comes to mind and crank out an essay without a second thought — or even a first thought. They don't care about learning anything new. All they want from their essay is for it to be finished — the sooner the better. I've had students actually *brag* to me that they never spend more than forty-five minutes on an essay.

Foolish student writers!

First, stop bragging about how little time you invest in your professor's class. Your professors might outwardly scoff at such bravado, but inwardly they weep. They sigh with sighs too deep for words.

Second, and more importantly, please understand that writing assignments are not blemishes on an otherwise happy life. Each writing assignment is in fact a generous invitation from your professor to spend some quality time with a new topic. Instead of giving you a lousy multiple-choice exam that will be graded by a machine, your professor has generously assigned your class an essay in the hope that at least a few of you will take this opportunity to actually get to know this new topic, to discover new ideas for yourselves, and to develop an understanding that will live beyond this assignment and probably your time in college.

Later, when the math and psychology professors stand around the Scantron machine, yukking it up while the machine grades your midterms, your writing professor will be loading up a painfully heavy briefcase with your essays and taking them home to read at a small desk in the laundry room while the rest of the family watches television or sleeps. It's a sacrifice of love, student writer, and your professors are willing to make that sacrifice because they care about your education.

You say you don't care about a particular topic? You think it's boring? That's because you don't yet understand why it matters to you — but it *does* matter to you because it is a part of the world you live in. Your professor understands this and is trying to help you see that for yourself with this writing assignment. All you have to do is receive the assignment as it was intended, as an opportunity to examine one small piece of the world more closely and share your ideas.

Most of this book focuses on the "share your ideas" part of the process, which in this case is writing a college essay. However, the college essay is really just a byproduct of the more important work of educating yourself about a topic. So before we work on how to share your ideas, we'll first look at how to educate yourself about your topic. We'll start with strategies for getting to know the topic. We'll then look at how to use questions to narrow your focus and consider more detailed information.

Step 1: Get to Know Your Topic

You begin the process of self-education by getting to know your topic. With most classes, you've already started to gather information about your topic by the time you receive a writing assignment. If you're taking American history, for example, you might be given a new topic to write about — Benjamin Franklin in Paris — but you've been learning about a lot of related topics from those Revolutionary times, so you're not completely unfamiliar with Franklin, Paris, or the relationship of the Colonial American and French governments.

What you already know will give you a few ideas about where you can gather more specific information about Franklin in Paris. But if you're not sure where to start, you also have a handy resource just standing there, idly, at the front of the classroom. Raise your hand, thank your professor for the assignment — in a sincere voice, please — and then ask for a few starting points for your research.

You have a couple of goals for this first step of self-education. One goal is to get a general sense of this topic. What is included here? How long was Franklin in Paris? Where did he live? What was he doing all that time? A second and more important goal is to look for the interesting subtopics within your topic. You must keep an eye out for anything that makes you curious to learn more because — soon! — you will narrow your focus to a subtopic and, not unexpectedly, learn more. You might as well narrow your focus to a subtopic that you would enjoy studying in more detail.

Begin with Reference Works

If you're too shy to talk to your professor, or if your professor is kind of scary, the best way to get started with a topic is to use general reference works. These publications are written by experts for an audience of non-experts. The experts are scholars who have studied this topic already and have an understanding about its size and makeup. The non-experts are you, the students.

General encyclopedias attempt to briefly explain *everything*. That's a starting point. Topical encyclopedias — an encyclopedia of religion or zoology or history, for example — are almost as ambitious, but they operate within the boundaries of that still-quite-large topic. They will give you a little more detailed information. Textbooks are another good option to consider. They provide a comprehensive overview of topics and explain technical terms. They're also good at presenting the debatable issues within your topic — any of which might become a good subtopic for deeper study.

The Internet is home to many useful reference works, too, but you can't just visit two or three websites and assume that you've mastered the topic. You've only scratched the surface of the topic, and what you've scratched could be garbage, too, depending on which two or three websites you visit. Using the Internet wisely means learning how to find credible websites and judge the reliability of any information you find. The reliability usually comes down to two factors — the credentials of the writers and the objectivity of the information.

With printed reference works, for example, the reliability is usually high. Any printed encyclopedia, for example, is the work of professional scholars.

These books have to be created by professionals or else libraries won't spend thousands of dollars to buy or rent them. Many online sources are also the careful work of trained professionals. Government websites, for example, are produced by agency professionals who understand their subject areas well. Many printed publications provide online versions of the same publication, and these are just as credible as the printed versions.

With some websites, however, the website's users create the content — book reviews, travel guides, dining reviews, technical help. These sites are less reliable because the writers are less credible. With a book review site, the writer of a review *might* be qualified to judge the quality of a book. But the reviewer might also be the still-angry former girlfriend of the writer. I've seen that happen firsthand. Or the reviewer might be an intern working for the book's publisher. User-generated sites rarely use editors to screen out dumb or biased reviews, so you have to be more careful judging the objectivity of each review. You can learn a lot at these sites, but you need to test what you learn with more objective sources.

"You can't just visit two or three websites and assume that you've mastered the topic. You've only scratched the surface of the topic, and what you've scratched could be garbage, too, depending on the website."

In the case of the popular online encyclopedia, *Wikipedia*, the content is provided by users, but there are several levels of editorial review and often fierce debate among competing viewpoints. That editorial review, along with citations of sources and a generally more informed set of contributors, makes this online encyclopedia more reliable than many professors are willing to admit. It's still possible for any idiot to corrupt an article with silly information — "Dogs are cats. Cats are dogs." — but that kind of silliness is quickly removed. However, even though *Wikipedia* is just about as reliable as printed encyclopedias, you still shouldn't trust it with all your heart. You need to check with other and probably more reliable sources to make sure you're getting good information.

The second quality to look for when it comes to reliability is objective information. That means you can actually see the details of the information — the number of feral pigdogs in Sacramento, the number of hours one congresswoman spends each week on fund-raising calls — and not just summaries of information or someone's opinion about what the information means.

Because the scope of a reference work is so broad, reference works don't have time to get into many details. The writers of these sources are usually credible professionals, so you might trust those summaries more than if they came from the users of a website, but they're not going to give you the detailed self-education you need. They're just a starting point.

If Your Topic Is a Text, Read It

If the assigned topic is a piece of writing — an essay by Kierkegaard, an article in the journal *Nature* — you have to get to know your topic by actually reading it. That sounds kind of obvious, doesn't it? Keep that in mind when you're tempted to turn to Internet summaries instead of reading the text yourself. Your professor assigned the text because she thinks you'll benefit from an understanding of it, so perhaps you should trust your professor's judgment this one time and get to know the text firsthand.

Reading the text once will help you get to know the topic — but just barely. Reading it once only gives you an acquaintance, not an understanding. In fact, you really need to read it twice just to become well acquainted. The first time lets you know what this is about in general. The second time through helps you to see the particulars.

As you go through the text — both times — make a few notes about things you notice. These might be great lines that you like, confusing phrases, information or events that don't make any sense, or anything else that stands out for you. When you can, try to state your notes as questions. Why plums? Where is her boyfriend while all of this is going on? Who is the "we" in this story?

Don't try to figure out the answers to all these questions while you're reading. That comes later. Just make notes so that you can later return to those questions and use them to narrow your focus within the text. Because once again, getting to know a topic is only your starting point when it comes to self-education. It's a required step, but you're doing this to find some interesting subtopic for further and deeper study.

Step 2: Narrow Your Focus

Narrowing your focus means looking more closely at a smaller part of your topic. The problem is that you can't explore *all* the complexities with a general topic. There's never enough time for that. So the solution is that you pick one small part of that general topic and then dig deeper into the details, the facts, and leave the rest of the broader topic for another time. Maybe.

Once you choose a narrower focus, you should more or less ignore the rest of the topic and become an expert about that question or subtopic. Doing so improves the odds of your essay becoming thoughtful, detailed, and engaging to readers. If you have any doubts about the appropriateness of a narrowed focus for an assignment, talk to your professor. He or she will be able to affirm your focus or help you find a better one.

With some writing assignments, you're assigned a question rather than a topic. In this case, your professor has narrowed the focus for you. This typically happens when the class has already spent some time with a general topic. Your professor now wants you to dig deeper into the information that's available so that you will understand it well enough to figure out a good answer to that question.

How to Find a Focus of Your Own

If no question has been assigned, then it's up to you to narrow your focus. The way to do that is to simply pay attention while you get to you know your topic. You'll find yourself drawn toward certain interesting or debatable or strange subtopics and questions. If you start with the broad topic of the United States Bill of Rights, for example, you might find yourself drawn to the Fifth Amendment — particularly the final "takings" clause. That's worth deeper exploration. Or if you are assigned the somewhat troubling topic of "mime," you might discover that Charlie Chaplin — whom you love — studied mime before becoming a film star. This raises the question of how much Chaplin's film performances rely on mime techniques. If that's a question you like, then go figure out a possible answer.

You might be drawn to these smaller parts of the topic because others have also found them interesting and have written about them. With a lot of complex issues — the effect of climate change on sea levels, for example, or whether a state can legalize a substance that the federal government has made illegal — people have a hard time agreeing about what all the information means. When you find a pocket of disagreement, it's easy to start digging deeper by reading the different positions others have taken and how they understand the information at hand.

The amazing thing is that *any* engaging focus will work. You might be drawn to it for personal reasons as you find connections between the topic and your own experience. You might be drawn to it by a professor who suggests that you might find this question interesting. You might flip open a textbook, jab your finger on a page, and find to your amazement that the paragraph you just jabbed is actually pretty interesting. It doesn't really matter how you get there. Just get there and you'll be fine.

What to Do When Nothing Engages You

With other writing assignments, you'll find that even after you've gotten to know the topic, nothing stands out as a potential narrow focus. In that case, you can use one of many writerly tricks to look more closely at the topic and see where your interests lie.

Free-writing, for example, is writing nonstop for fifteen or twenty minutes to see what your subconscious mind can come up with. We're all so repressed and conflicted that there are usually several interesting observations or questions ready to escape from the painful confines of our brains. Mind-mapping is using a chart of some sort to visually divide a topic into its many subtopics — and then sub-subtopics and sub-sub-subtopics. This helps you identify interesting patterns or components that might be worth a closer look.

Another useful device is the reporter's questions, the six questions that any good journalist will ask to explore a topic: Who? What? When? Where? Why? and How? These questions help you explore and understand the specifics of your topic, and this process almost always raises additional questions that will lead you to further exploration.

Who? Who is doing this? To whom is it being done? Who else is affected? You can think of this question as identifying the actors in a drama. The drama is your topic, and the actors are the forces at work within that topic. The actors involved might be human or they might be social factors (unemployment, inflation) or groups (the NRA, unruly schoolchildren) or nations or ideas — anyone or anything that might do something or cause something to happen.

What? What happened? What is happening? What is going to happen? These might be physical, observable events or internal, unobservable events. Think about change with this question. What changed? What is changing? What will change? One technique here is to take each of the answers to "Who?" and look for some verbs that go with each noun (unemployment increases incidents of spousal abuse, the NRA lobbies against gun registration).

When? This might be a specific time or date. It might also be the set of conditions that must be present for an event to happen, like the circumstances that must be present for the stock market to crash or for a yucca plant to bloom.

Where? This question can look at actual physical locations in which an event might take place — the city, the house, the sandbox where the cat has been seen digging. However, it also considers less tangible contexts, such as the country music scene, the Internet, or the fast-food industry.

Why? What causes this to happen? This is one of the more useful questions because it forces you to start figuring out why your "who" actors are doing the "what" actions, or why your "what" actions have such interesting consequences. You make more sense of the topic by considering the relationship of actors to other actors and events to other events. When you try to answer this question, use complete sentences that include the word "because." Using the word "because" forces you to at least guess about why something happens. And guessing is fine, too. It gives you ideas you can test with more detailed information about that smaller part of the topic.

How? This question looks at method, at how something happens. It's another good question that will help you to make connections and explore beneath the surface of a topic. You should try to answer this question with complete sentences, too. Using the word "by" in your sentences will help you note or guess about the methods used by the actors.

By focusing on the particulars of a topic, the reporter's questions tend to generate deeper consideration than free-writing or mind-mapping. Doing this will almost always lead to questions or aspects of the topic that you hadn't thought of before. And that's where the fun begins.

Step 3: Research the Narrowed Focus

Once you've narrowed your focus, it's time to leave the wading pool and head over to the big pool. That means setting aside the reference works and spending time with more detailed and objective sources of information. These include books, serious popular magazines, newspapers, and scholarly journals. These sources help you to educate yourself about your newly narrowed topic more thoroughly. They allow you to get your hands on actual facts. You will then see the topic for what it is and not through the eyes of someone else's summaries.

You can find a few of these resources online and available to the general public, but the best way for student writers to get their hands on serious and scholarly information is through a college or university library. Campus libraries now use electronic databases to catalog their resources, so you can find what you need using key word searches — not unlike how you look for information with an Internet search engine.

Turn Questions Into Key Word Searches

To find more comprehensive information from library databases, you need to search for it using key words. The key words will come from the questions you have. Suppose you have this question: "Did Ben Franklin contract syphilis while serving as an American diplomat in Paris?" To create a list of key words for your search, you simply circle the important words in your question — Ben Franklin, syphilis, American diplomat, Paris. You then search for books or articles by typing some or all of those terms into a database search page.

That's your starting point, and that might be all you have to do to find the information you need about Franklin's sexual activity. However, you might also find that those terms generate a list of a thousand articles, which is more than you have time to review, or that those articles are only loosely related to the American diplomat. On the other hand, you might also find that searching for those terms gives you a list of zero possible sources. That seems pretty unlikely with some topics and some questions, but it happens all the time if the key words you use aren't the same ones that the database uses.

One way to improve your search is to try using synonyms for some of your terms. Instead of "diplomat," you could use "statesman," "ambassador," or "envoy." Instead of "American," you could use "Colonial" or "Colonial American." By trying different synonyms, you often stumble upon the key words that best fit your topic from the database's perspective. Write those down so you can keep using them.

A recent student, for example, was doing research about exotic dancers, but she couldn't find any scholarly articles using the terms "exotic dancers," "strippers," or anything else she could think of. Working with a reference librarian, she found that the preferred synonym in the databases was "stripteasers." Who'd have thought it? When she used "stripteasers," she found forty years' worth of scholarly data, which was also a bit of a surprise.

Another thing you can try is using broader search terms. Instead of "syphilis," for example, you might use "sexually transmitted diseases" or "venereal disease" to enlarge your search. Instead of "Paris" you might search for "France" or "Europe." In this way, you will sometimes find articles with a broader scope that also include some useful information about your question, even if they don't focus on it. This is good for finding scholarly books. They're almost always going to be more broadly focused than you need simply because of their length. However, within those books you might find chapters or parts of chapters that will be useful.

Build Your Understanding with Serious Popular Articles

When you search your library's databases for scholarly information, the results will be much better than when you search the Internet. When you look at the results, there won't be any defunct websites in the mix. There won't be any ads for free laptops or baldness remedies or attractive singles in your area. When you search for information at the library, that's exactly what you'll find — information — and most of it will be reliable because librarians have no patience for unreliable information. They root it out of there like so many angry badgers.

As you begin reading the articles that you've located, it's a good idea to start with the more serious popular sources on your list — *The Economist*, *The Atlantic Monthly*, *The Christian Science Monitor*, and so on. These magazines make their money by targeting popular issues and exploring them thoughtfully and in detail. This brings more educated readers to their pages, and then they can sell advertising to businesses that want to reach readers with higher levels of education and thus — usually — higher incomes.

> "Don't confuse serious popular magazines with the far more popular and far less serious magazines that focus on the sad lives of glamorous celebrities or how to make your wedding even more expensive."

Serious popular sources are so useful for you as a self-educator because they translate the detailed work of scholars into language that any educated person can understand. They also focus on smaller parts of the topic than general reference works, so they provide more detailed and more timely information.

But don't confuse serious popular magazines with the far more popular and far less serious magazines that focus on the sad lives of glamorous celebrities or how to make your wedding even more expensive. These magazines are popular because they try to entertain as many readers as possible. They can then charge more for advertising that reaches a bajillion readers. That's fine. I have nothing against entertainment or advertising. But when it comes to educating yourself about a topic, the serious popular magazines have much better information to offer.

Newspapers are the most common type of serious popular publication. They rely on professional journalists to gather information from credible sources, to confirm the validity of that information, and to present that information objectively. They cover a wide array of events, usually in brief articles. With compelling or controversial events, they often explore the details in more depth, including information from scholars, local authorities, and others who have a professional relationship to the topic. That can provide valuable information about ongoing events.

Not all newspapers are credible, of course. Tabloid papers, for example, often ignore real-world information and print speculation because they are run by and for knuckleheads. They also like to focus on the lurid details that appeal to the fears and lusts of their readers. That's why they're so popular — fear and lust sells papers. And unfortunately, the success of tabloids has led more serious newspapers to start imitating their tactics just to survive in this strange world of ours.

Deepen Your Understanding with Scholarly Works

At the deep end of the information pool, you will find articles that are written by scholars, edited by scholars, and, for the most part, read by scholars. Some of these sources are books published by university presses. Most of them are articles published in academic journals.

Scholarly works are the most credible for two reasons. First, the writers are knowledgeable about their field because that's what they do for a living. They're also trained in methods of gathering and testing information within that field. In addition, when a scholar submits an article or book for publication by an academic journal or publisher, other scholars are hired to examine that submission, judge its value, and sniff out even the smallest flaws — just itching for some reason to reject it. Anything that does get published has to hold up well to that kind of jealous scrutiny.

What makes scholarly works most valuable, however, is that they focus most directly on the details of information. This allows readers to see those details for themselves and form their own conclusions about what it all means. These details are measurable facts rather than the summary or interpretation of facts that show up in newspapers and magazines. They are direct quotations from primary texts, the quantifiable results of experiments or studies, and the exact words of interviewees. Scholarly works present the writers' conclusions about these topics, but those conclusions are then backed up with facts from the real world. That's what makes this information more objective and useful.

For all their virtues, however, scholarly sources have one major drawback. Scholars write these articles for other scholars. They don't mess around trying to explain things to newbies like you or me. They assume that their readers are familiar with the topic and the terminology of their discipline.

If you're not familiar with the topic or terminology — and there's a good chance you're not, student writer — you will find scholarly sources difficult to read and even more difficult to understand. That's not a reason to avoid them, however. That's a reason to be patient with your climb up the learning curve. It's also a reason to go back to your general sources — especially those topical dictionaries and textbooks — for help decoding the language of difficult articles and books.

Write More about Less

At first, you might not feel comfortable narrowing the focus of your research. It does, after all, violate the simple math of high school writing:

size of topic = length of paper

However, here's one of those writerly paradoxes for you. As it turns out, a broad focus actually tends to *limit* the writer. It tends to generate a dull and shorter-than-expected essay. This happens because the broad range of information within a broad topic forces you to rely on summarized rather than detailed information. Summaries can be written quickly — just a few words. And once the information has been summarized, the only way to make a paper longer is to repeat yourself. That's boring for you, and it's even worse for your readers. Summaries are dull, too, unless they're illustrated by details. So when the focus is broad, you end up with an short, dull essay.

Suppose that your topic is math and your essay answers the question of how important math is in daily life. With a focus like this, you'll need to include a book-sized amount of information because almost every aspect of daily life has a direct or indirect connection to math. You might offer a few detailed examples — balancing a checkbook, figuring out what kind of mileage your SUV gets — but the examples won't adequately explain your answer to the question because they cover only a small part of daily life. To answer the question fully, you'll need to cover all of the math-related aspects of daily life, and that will require summaries of the broad range of information that's needed. You'll end up with paragraphs like this:

> Math is also important in household activities. Math may be used to balance the checkbook and make budgets. It may also be used to determine the cost of vacations or weekend trips. It may be used when shopping to compare the relative cost of similar products and help determine the most economical product to purchase. With just about every household activity, math is close at hand!

The summaries in this paragraph cover a lot of information quickly, but that doesn't help you get the length you want and need. More importantly, they don't spark your imagination or provide any sparks for your readers because there aren't any details here for readers to imagine. The broader focus gives you more information to work with, but you can see that covering a lot of information with summaries won't result in a longer or even interesting essay. Yes, math is close at hand, but we already knew that. The idea isn't worthy of that sad little exclamation point.

When you narrow your focus, you remove information from consideration, and although that might make you feel a little squeamish about the length of the paper, it's still a step in the right direction. By removing information from consideration, you're able to give closer consideration to the small pot of information that remains. You can get into the details. By narrowing "How important is math in daily life?" to "How important is geometry in daily life?" you eliminate from consideration all forms of math except geometry. By narrowing your focus further to "How important is plane geometry in residential construction?" you remove most of the original topic and finally get into some detailed information. You might explore how the Pythagorean theorem, for example, is used by framing carpenters to make sure walls are laid out square:

> One common use of plane geometry occurs whenever a framing carpenter needs to plan where to put the walls of a house. It's essential that the walls are square (that is, with the junction of walls forming true right angles). This makes the work of drywallers and finish carpenters much easier because they will be able to make all their cuts quickly without having to take the time to compensate for walls and corners that aren't square. To make sure the walls are all laid out square, the framer uses the Pythagorean theorem: $A^2 + B^2 = C^2$. If Wall A, for example, is 30 feet long, then A^2 will be 900. If Wall B is 40 feet long, then B^2 will be 1600. If Wall A and Wall B are joined at a true right angle, then the distance from the far end of Wall A to the far end of Wall B will be the square root of the sum of 900 and 1600. The sum of 900 plus 1600 is 2500. The square root of 2500 is 50. If Wall A and Wall B are laid out square, the diagonal that connects their far ends would be 50 feet long. If the framer makes sure these lengths are true, the walls will be square.

If math gives you stomachaches, then this detailed example of math for the carpenter isn't going to do much for you — except give you a stomachache, of course. But even then, while you hold your aching belly and moan, you can still appreciate how the specific information gets its narrow little point across more clearly than you saw in the previous summary with its huge ideas. Here you have details that you can visualize in your mind.

You can also see that it took a lot of sentences to present these specific details. A *lot* of sentences. In fact, even though it does use a lot of detailed information, this math paragraph is still a little rushed. It could have walked through the process in even more detail with the illustration of a hypothetical carpenter at work on a hypothetical house.

Digging into the details of your narrowed focus is where educating yourself offers the greatest rewards. This thoughtful consideration of detailed information offers the only meaningful reward you're going to get from a writing assignment. The essay you eventually write will come and go. The grade will become unimportant almost immediately. But when you take the time to really educate yourself about your topic, that topic will stay with you — especially the part of the topic that you explore more deeply.

As an added bonus, narrowing your focus also prepares you to write an engaging and effective essay. Because you understand the topic so well, the length of the essay won't be a problem for you. You'll be able to find an idea of your own that will be worth sharing with readers, and you'll be able to share that idea with sophisticated explanations and detailed information.

The Big Ideas

This chapter took a closer look at the first step in the writing process — educating yourself about a topic. The actual purpose of any college writing assignment is for you to learn something, and in the long run, whatever you teach yourself is what you will have to show for your labors, too. These are the big ideas that will guide your self-education:

1. Get to know your topic: Use reference works, textbooks, newspapers, and professors to become familiar with a topic in general. If the topic is a text, read it.

2. Narrow your focus: This is one of the keys to successful writing. To write well, you have to write with detailed information. To get to detailed information, you have to dig deep into the particulars of a topic. To dig deep, you have to only focus at one narrow part of a topic.

3. Research the narrowed focus: Use more reliable and more detailed sources of information to research the details of your narrowed topic. Use a reference librarian at first, too. They are like training wheels for new researchers, and I think that we can all agree that training wheels make a lot of sense when you're first starting out.

4. Less is more: Focusing on a narrow part of a topic (less) allows you to write about it in greater detail (more). Don't be afraid, student writer. Your paper will be long enough.

Chapter 8
Find and Improve Your Main Idea

Once you get used to the process of educating yourself about a topic, you'll find that gathering and considering information becomes surprisingly enjoyable. But there is a danger in this — there's danger in everything, I suppose, if you look for it. The danger is that you'll get so excited about the new information that you start writing your paper without first processing all this new information, wringing all the information into a paper like so much water from a sponge. Those papers are fun to write, but they're a mess for readers because the purpose of the paper — your thesis — is unclear. Your readers aren't sure why you're sharing all this information.

With formal writing, you have to know what you're writing about before you start writing. You'll probably resist investing much time in this step of the writing process — everyone does — but that doesn't make it any less essential. To write an effective essay, you need to figure out what all that information means. You have to find and improve your main idea. That's how it becomes a part of you and not just facts that you dump into a paper and forget.

This chapter will show you how to do that.

Find a Legitimate Main Idea

To write a college essay, you first need to know what your main idea will be, and you need to know this precisely. You can't *kind of* know. If you only *kind of* know what your idea is, then your readers will only *kind of* know what you mean. Transmitting a vague understanding in an essay is not to be confused with success. It will lead to confused readers and comments from your professor such as, "I'm not sure what you mean by this" and "D."

The best way to identify and refine the main idea of your future essay is to put it into words and then refine it as a more precise and accurate idea.

To do this, you need to use a thesis statement. You remember this term from chapter 1, right? A thesis statement is a one-sentence explanation of your main idea. It might look something like this:

> People should try to laugh when they feel stressed out, even if it's fake laughter, because any kind of laughter will help to reduce stress.

Let me point out a few things about this thesis statement. First, this thesis statement is a complete sentence. That's good. You need a complete sentence to have a complete thought. Second, it defines an opinion — advice is always an opinion. That's good, too, because an opinion is the essential ingredient for an essay. Third, it includes a reason why readers should follow the advice, so we know what the essay will need to explain in order to defend the idea. The sentence thus captures the entire future essay. With this taped to your computer monitor, you'd know exactly what you needed to write.

The thesis statement we're talking about in this chapter is a *writerly* thesis statement. We use it to clarify our thinking before we write the essay — not to introduce the idea to readers in the opening paragraph like you saw in chapter 2. The writerly thesis statement is a writer's tool. It works behind the scenes to help you capture and improve your main idea while your thoughts are still fluid. It then guides you while you write, helping you to stick to one main idea. This leads to more successful papers, better grades, higher-paying jobs, and the admiration of friends and family.

In spite of these obvious rewards, many student writers still think that the writerly thesis statement is a complete waste of time. Wouldn't it be easier, they think, to just write the paper once they have a general direction and all the information is still fresh?

Foolish student writers!

It only *seems* like a complete waste of time because the quality of your thinking has never mattered before. But the success of a college essay — both personally and academically — depends on the quality of your own ideas, not on your ability to collect information. By capturing your idea in advance, the writerly thesis statement allows you to fix the any weaknesses in your idea before your weak idea turns into a weak essay. It's one of the most valuable tools you have as a writer.

How to Develop a Useful Thesis Statement

Starting is often the hardest step in using the thesis statement to identify and improve an idea. It's hard to write a single sentence that clearly states your main idea. It's much easier to write a paragraph or two. It's even easier to let your idea remain a vague notion floating around on your brain waves. Consequently, there is a tendency among student writers to work on main ideas "mentally," often while watching television or sleeping.

However, one of the great writerly secrets is that *any* starting point is a good starting point. Once you've written a sentence — even a lousy one — you can tinker with it to make it better, and tinkering is easier than starting. Take this lousy starting point, for example:

the stress-reducing benefits of laughter

The reason it's lousy is that it's just a phrase — not a grammatical sentence. If what you write down is a phrase rather than a complete sentence, then even if it's a nice little phrase like this, you've stated a topic or subtopic rather than a complete idea. This phrase tells readers what you will be writing about — the stress-reducing benefits of laughter — but it doesn't state your own opinion about those benefits. To state your opinion, you'll need a complete sentence. Try again:

Will laughter reduce your stress?

I probably should have mentioned that when I say "grammatical sentence," I don't mean a question, even though that's also a grammatical sentence. Questions ask for ideas. They don't present them. The *answer* to this question might be a reasonable opinion of your own, but to capture that thought, you'll need to state an assertion rather than a question. Try again:

I think that laughter often reduces stress.

Now that is a grammatical sentence. The subject is "I," and the predicate is "think that laughter often reduces stress." It's a statement rather than a question. The statement also captures a discovery of yours, which is great. You are definitely heading in the right direction, student writer.

But look at the subject of the sentence — "I." Having "I" as the subject implies that this is an idea about you. And because the main verb is "think," the idea is that you are having a thought. That's not the idea you're going to write about. "I think" also suggests that you are qualifying this idea by saying that it's just your opinion, that this seems true to you but you really don't want to get into a big fight over it. That's not what's going on here, either. You've done your research. You have reasons for believing in this idea.

College writing requires you to present an opinion of your own, so the "I think" is already understood. Your opinion must also be more than just a hunch of yours, an idea that shouldn't have to be qualified by a wimpy "I think." This is a reasonable opinion, an idea that is based on the information you considered when you were exploring your narrowed focus. It needs to be an idea that makes sense not just to you but to anyone who looks at the information.

So try again, emboldened student writer, and this time let your topic become the subject of the sentence:

Laughter often reduces stress.

Much better! Now you have a complete sentence. It's an assertion of your own idea. It focuses on a specific topic. It doesn't back away with an unnecessary "I think." This is a big step forward. You've identified a potential main idea for an essay. Nice work.

In a minute we'll look at how to improve that idea before you write the essay. First, though, let's look at some thesis statements that will lead to reports rather than essays. If what you write down is a sentence that summarizes information or states a fact about the topic, then even though it is a grammatical sentence and a statement, it's not a good main idea for an essay. Consider these examples:

Laughter is a regular part of human life.

Most people have some degree of stress.

These are both statements, but they are statements of fact rather than opinion. We already accept these ideas as true. If you write about these ideas, you'll be writing a report about information rather than an essay about your interpretation of what the information means. Unless you are supposed to write a report, your writerly thesis statement should capture an opinion.

And while we're talking about less-than-desirable writerly thesis statements, understand that you're not much better off with an opinion that is obvious, like this:

> Laughter is a great gift.

That's not a fact or a summary of information, so it *could* become the main idea of an essay. However, this idea is so simple that any ten-year-old could figure it out — if ten-year-olds didn't already have better things to do. The essay that explains this idea, even if it's technically excellent, will have little to offer its readers. More importantly, you won't get anything out of this process but a so-so grade. You can do better than this, student writer, and you should — for your sake and for the sake of the poor, weak-eyed professor who assigned the essay.

Use a Thesis Statement to Improve Your Main Idea

One fairly easy and effective way to improve your main idea and make sure it's worth the effort is to improve your writerly thesis statement. You can use the thesis statement to make your thinking more precise, and you can use it to make sure that the idea is accurate.

Make Your Idea More Precise

Let's take that idea you had about laughter as an example:

> Laughter often reduces stress.

To make an idea more precise, you need to define the key terms of the thesis statement more clearly. So what do you mean by "laughter"? What do you mean by "reduces"? What do you mean by "stress"? Try to be more precise:

> Laughing out loud often lowers emotional stress.

That's a little better. Now we know that you're talking about laughing out loud. We also see that you're focusing on the emotional stress that people feel, rather than physical or financial or other kinds of stress. But what about "lower"? That's really just another way of saying "reduces," isn't it? So how much does it lower the stress? What did the information tell you about this?

If your answer to a question like this is "I don't know," then you have a problem that you need to take seriously. If you don't know what you mean, then you don't have any business presenting this idea in an essay. You're just guessing. You either need to go back to your topic and educate yourself more thoroughly, or you need to move on to a different idea of yours that is not a guess.

And by the way, indignant student writer, it's a poor excuse to say that the source you were using didn't tell you how much the stress was reduced. It probably didn't go into the details because it was a general reference article or a magazine article. General sources of information stick to the surface of a topic. When you run into sources that aren't as detailed as you need them to be, it's *your* job to find more detailed information, not theirs. You know it's out there because the writers of the general sources were able to find it and summarize it. So go find the information — or go find a reference librarian and then the information — and come back with a new thesis statement:

Laughing out loud often lowers emotional stress by 20-30%.

Good job with the follow-up research. Now you know more precisely what you mean by "lower." But that "often" still needs to be considered. I'll go out on a limb and say it's in the sentence because you know that this stress reduction doesn't always happen. There are exceptions to this rule, and "often" covers those exceptions without you having to explain just how often it happens. It was nice of "often" to save you that effort, but it leaves your sentence imprecise. So replace the "often" with a statement that includes the exceptions to this idea. Try again:

Except in the cases of severely depressed people, laughing out loud lowers emotional stress by 20-30%.

Now that's what I call less imprecise.

Make Sure Your Idea Is Accurate

Before you get to the planning and writing of your essay, however, you still have to make sure that your idea is accurate. That means testing whether the idea you're asserting in this thesis statement is founded on sufficient reasons or information. The quickest way to test this is to add the word "because" to your sentence and then summarize what leads you to believe this idea is valid. Try it for yourself:

> Except in the cases of severely depressed people, laughing out loud lowers emotional stress by 20-30% because laughing out loud releases a powerful mood-enhancing chemical into the bloodstream.

Precision still matters, so you might as well name the chemical while you're at it:

> Except in the cases of severely depressed people, laughing out loud lowers emotional stress by 20-30% because laughing out loud releases serotonin into the bloodstream.

Now you can work on accuracy, and you do that by going back to the information you used to educate yourself and judge whether that information truly and sufficiently supports the main idea. And here's the first thing to understand about that — it probably doesn't.

You see, student writer, life is large, and we are small. No matter how skilled we become at gathering and analyzing information, there's always much, much, *much* more information that we don't see and don't understand. So as you consider information and draw your conclusions, you — like all humans — must be cautious about what you claim the information teaches. You must be humble, so to speak.

One way to judge whether your information provides enough support is to turn that writerly thesis statement into a kind of math problem. Imagine that the "because" is an equals sign. Does the idea that you state before the "because" equal the information or reasons that you state after the "because"? If it does, then your statement is accurate. If it doesn't, then you need to tinker with one or both sides of the equation so that the idea and its support balance out. Let's take a look:

Except in the cases of severely depressed people, laughing out loud lowers emotional stress by 20-30%	= (because)	laughing out loud releases serotonin into the bloodstream

With this sentence, the question is whether your information about serotonin being released into the bloodstream is strong enough information to support this assertion about laughter. I want to think the best of you, so I will assume that you found this information in the library, and that it came from a scholarly article. Let's pretend that what you found was a study from Purdue University researchers. As information goes, scholarly studies like this are usually credible. And Purdue has a nice ring to it.

But does this study *prove* that this idea is true? No, it doesn't. There are two problems. First, because this is just a study of a limited number of humans, all it can do is identify a pattern in those humans that might be true in all humans. Second, the study focuses on the chemical, not the stress, so the connection of serotonin to stress reduction still needs to be made. The study is still worth considering, but it doesn't prove that laughter will for a fact reduce stress except in certain circumstances.

So even though the information makes sense and suggests that laughter really is beneficial, you shouldn't take it too far by saying this study proves something that it only *suggests* might be true. To make your statement of the idea accurate, then, you have to capture this suggestive nature of the supporting information:

> Except in the cases of severely depressed people, laughing out loud appears to lower emotional stress by 20-30% because laughing out loud releases serotonin into the bloodstream.

That's better. By adding "appears to," you've turned this idea from a fact into a possibility. It now appears — there's that word again — that the idea is equal to its support. Thanks mostly to all your hard work and partially to all my nagging, the thesis statement is now more precise and more accurate. Now you're ready to turn your attention to the next step — writing.

The Value of the Writerly Thesis Statement

Working so intently on one single sentence might feel difficult or overly time-consuming at first. You just have to get started with a simple idea — even a lousy one. From there, you can clean the idea up and expand it into a complex idea. You have to take your time as you look at each word and make it more precise. You also have to stay grounded in the information you've learned about your topic and use it to make the statement accurate. That's not that hard to do. It's really just a matter of choosing to make some time for it.

But I'll be honest with you. A lot of student writers blow this chapter off and launch into their essays like everything I've told them is a load of manure. "Thank you, Mr. English Teacher," they imply by their actions, "but I've been writing papers for years. I don't need your *writerly* thesis statements." They have more faith in their own ability to crank out essays without any planning than they do in the thesis statement's ability to prepare them to write thoughtful essays.

Foolish student writers!

I understand that inspiration will sometimes bail you out in spite of poor planning. Creative phrasing might decorate sloppy thinking just enough to make it appear thoughtful. A professor might read a stack of papers late at night while watching a zombie movie, half-drunk, miserable for company — and in this way miss the fact that you haven't said anything worth sharing. Line up enough accidents of fate, student writer, and it's still possible for you to get by without investing any time into a writerly thesis statement.

However, you will eventually come to a place where you need to make sure your idea is precise and accurate before you present it in written form. It might not be a college essay, either. It might be a letter of resignation, a business plan, a scholarship application — something that needs to be taken seriously. When that day comes, remember this little chapter. The thesis statement will still be a useful tool for you, and this chapter will still be here, too, reminding you how to use it — as long as you don't sell the book back to the bookstore at the end of the term.

The Big Ideas

Student writers often fill their brains with information during the first step of the writing process and then jump right to presenting that information without figuring out what it means or what their main idea will be. That's why this second step in the writing process is important. It provides you with a clear direction for everything that follows.

Here are the key ideas related to Step 2 of the writing process:

1. The writerly thesis statement: This planning tool is the best way for you to define and refine the main idea of your future essay. It allows — or maybe forces — you to take a close look at your main idea before you do any writing so that when you do begin to write, you have an idea that's worth sharing with others.

2. Any starting point is a good starting point: Once you've written down a thesis statement — even a lousy one — you can tinker with it to make it better. Tinkering is easier than starting. Tinkering with writing is also more effective than trying to figure it out mentally.

3. Improve your idea with the writerly thesis statement: One way to improve your main idea is to make the words of your thesis statement more precise. A second way to improve it is to make sure the words are accurate, that you don't claim more than your evidence supports.

4. This is worth your while: Why would I lie to you? If I say that the writerly thesis statement is valuable to you, student writer, it's because I've seen its value with student after student for decades. Just try it. See for yourself.

Chapter 9
Plan the Body of Your Essay

For the moment, we'll ignore the opening and closing of your essay. Many student writers enjoy spending long, desperate hours staring at a blank computer screen, waiting for a perfect first line to appear from somewhere in the universe. If you enjoy staring at a blank computer screen, you still can, of course. It's peaceful. I get that.

However, when it comes to writing your essay, it's a lot more effective to write a great opening *after* you've written the body of the essay. At that point, you have a better idea of what you need to introduce. You also know what ideas and information you'll need to summarize in the closing. So for now, the opening and closing can wait.

In this chapter, we'll look at how to plan the body of your essay before you write it. To do that, you have to remember all the way back to chapter 2 that essays are made of paragraphs, and that every formal paragraph presents one main — supporting — idea of its own. That supporting idea is stated by the topic sentence of the paragraph. The same idea is then explained in detail by the supporting sentences in that paragraph. Remember that? Life sure was a lot simpler back in chapter 2.

We're going to talk about body paragraphs in this chapter, so if that idea has become a little hazy, you might want to first reread chapter 2. You paid good money for chapter 2, after all. You might as well read it twice.

Build a Topic Sentence Outline Beforehand

A topic sentence outline is simply a list of the topic sentences for your essay's future body paragraphs. It helps you plan your essay by forcing you to decide what paragraphs you will write and what each paragraph will explain. If you invested some time in developing a precise, writerly thesis statement, you're ready to do this. However, you have to break the topic sentence outline process into steps or else it becomes a little overwhelming.

Let's take a look at the topic sentence outline for the *Jane Eyre* essay from chapter 2. Each supporting idea is numbered, and if it takes two paragraphs to present an idea, I add an "a" or "b." Here's the result:

1. One early example of this error in judgment comes from chapter 1 when Jane has a fight with her cousin, John Reed.

2a. In spite of these fairly severe consequences, Jane makes the same basic mistake soon after her red-room experience.

2b. This time, the consequences for Jane's mistake are more severe than a trip to the red-room or dinner by herself.

3a. Before Jane leaves Gateshead, she makes the same mistake one last time by attacking her aunt directly.

3b. The consequences for Jane's third mistake are the most severe.

4. It would take a paper as long as this novel to cover all the times Jane makes this mistake because from start to finish, she refuses to think things through when her heart is aroused by any kind of strong feeling.

You can see how this provides the student writer with a clear plan to follow while drafting the body of the essay. But what you see above is the finished product — not the starting point. The student writer didn't sit down and create this outline while eating a light lunch. The starting point was chaos and confusion. The topic is 220 pages of a Charlotte Brontë novel, for crying out loud — way too much information! And the focus isn't much better. What was the main character's single biggest mistake? In 220 pages, there are *dozens* of mistakes to choose from. As the student writer considered all the possibilities, she raised her eyes to heaven and cried out in anguish, "Why?! Why?!"

But then the student writer remembered how to take control of the situation — to build a topic sentence outline. And even more fortunately, she remembered to build that outline one step at a time. Life became worth living again. She was able to finish her light lunch.

Let's take a look at the steps she took to build this outline.

Step 1: List Your Evidence

The first step in building a topic sentence is actually pretty easy. All you have to do is list the relevant evidence you have — the same information or ideas that helped you to form your opinion about this topic. If the information helped you to make up your mind, then it will help your readers to make up their minds, too.

While working on this essay, the student writer created a long list of mistakes that Jane Eyre makes:

1. Jane calls her cousin John a bad person. — reprimanded by aunt

2. Jane punches her cousin John and calls all the Reeds bad. — sent to red-room (where she freaks out), isolated from other children

3. Jane tells off her aunt for being a hypocrite. — removed from Gateshead (immediately), kept from rich uncle (later)

4. Jane crawls into bed with her dying best friend. — puts herself (and others) in harm's way

5. Jane wanders around the swamps barefoot all winter. — puts herself (and others) in harm's way, isolates herself

6. Jane abruptly leaves her teaching position for the first governess position that comes open. — puts herself in a vulnerable position, isolated from others

7. Jane unquestionably obeys Rochester and doesn't tell anyone about "Grace Poole" when there is a fire. — isolates herself from others at Thornfield, makes herself even more dependent on Rochester

8. Jane unquestionably obeys Rochester and doesn't tell anyone about the "Grace Poole's" attack on Mason. — further isolates herself from others at Thornfield, makes herself even more dependent on Rochester

9. Jane blows off Mrs. Fairfax's warnings about Rochester. — makes herself dependent on Rochester, isolated, vulnerable

At this point, the student writer starts to hyperventilate a little because that's a *lot* of evidence to present. Explaining all of these mistakes and their consequences will take many more pages that the assignment allows or the student desires to write. But this abundance of evidence is a good thing. It means she can make wise choices about what evidence to include and what to leave out.

That brings our student to Step 2.

Step 2: Prioritize

Which pieces of evidence will do the best job of showing readers what you think and why your ideas are good ones? That's the question for Step 2.

Our student writer's thesis is that Jane keeps making the same mistake over and over — acting without thinking. As she considers her list of nine examples of this mistake, she finds that the most obvious examples are the early ones because the actions and the consequences are so tangible:

1. Jane calls her cousin John a bad person. — reprimanded by aunt

2. Jane punches her cousin John and calls all the Reeds bad. — sent to the red-room, isolated from other children

3. Jane tells off her aunt for being a hypocrite. — removed from Gateshead (immediately), kept from rich uncle (later)

She might move punching cousin John up to number one as the most tangible of Jane's mistakes, but otherwise, nothing changes. The first three examples remain the most tangible.

The next items in the ranked list are tangible actions whose consequences aren't quite so tangible:

4. Jane crawls into bed with her dying best friend. — puts herself (and others) in harm's way

5. Jane wanders around the swamps barefoot all winter. — puts herself (and others) in harm's way, isolates herself

The later mistakes on the list of evidence are more serious, but they are also less tangible. They are errors of judgment — trusting the wrong person and not trusting the right person — rather than physical actions. The consequences are also less tangible — social isolation, emotional dependence. If our student writer ranked Jane Eyre's mistakes by seriousness, these should come first, but because she is ranking them by how well they tangibly illustrate the general problem of thoughtlessness, these are a low priority. So our student writer ends up with this prioritized list of evidence:

Most Tangible
1. Jane calls John names
2. Jane punches John
3. Jane tells off Mrs. Reed

Less Tangible
4. Jane gets in bed with dying Helen
5. Jane wanders through swamps

Not Very Tangible
6. Jane leaves Lowood to be a governess
7. Jane keeps quiet about the fire
8. Jane keeps quiet about the attack on Mason
9. Jane blows off Mrs. Fairfax's warnings

Now it's time to translate that into an outline of actual paragraphs.

Step 3: Outline Paragraph Topics

With any form of writing, the importance of an idea translates into the number of sentences that you give it. The more important the idea is, the more sentences you dedicate to its explanation. In the body of your essay, then, the most important ideas are what you should write about most — many sentences, several paragraphs. The less important ideas should be summarized with fewer sentences — or dropped entirely.

Your most important ideas should all have their own paragraphs. If one paragraph won't allow you to explain an idea in detail, then you may need to explain it over two or more paragraphs. Smaller ideas can be combined into umbrella paragraphs or left out entirely.

Using the prioritized list of topics, our student writer can now plan out the paragraphs in the body:

1. Jane calls John names (action) and gets reprimanded (consequence).

That's a fairly brief and simple incident, so it can be covered in detail in just one paragraph.

The next errors are more complicated, however, so our student writer decided to divide them in half — one paragraph for the mistake and a second for the consequences:

2a. Jane punches John (action).

2b. Jane is sent to the red-room, isolated from others (consequence).

3a. Jane tells off Mrs. Reed (action).

3b. Jane is sent away, deprived of her rich uncle (consequence).

The body of the essay is up to five paragraphs now, and our student writer has a math midterm on Thursday, so the rest of these ideas will have to go into a single, mostly summarizing paragraph:

4. Jane continues making mistakes
    a. At Lowood
        i.   Jane gets in bed with dying Helen.
        ii. Jane wanders through swamps.
    b. At Thornfield
        i.   Jane leaves Lowood to be a governess.
        ii. Jane keeps quiet about the fire.
        iii. Jane keeps quiet about the attack on Mason.
        iv. Jane blows off Mrs. Fairfax's warnings.

This is a nice set of paragraphs for the body of the essay. The first five present Jane's general mistake with lots of tangible details. The sixth paragraph uses summarized information to show that the pattern continues throughout the first half of the novel.

If you put it all together, what does it add up to? That's right. It adds up to the thesis. That's what you were going to say, wasn't it? This set of paragraphs and the evidence they present collectively explain the student writer's main idea and demonstrate that the idea is based on actual evidence from the novel.

Step 4: Organize the Paragraphs

As you saw in chapter 2, everything makes more sense when it's organized. So now it's time to organize the body paragraphs so readers will be able to see how this information fits together. We'll talk in more detail about organization later in this chapter. For now, we'll look just at how this student writer has organized these particular paragraphs.

Because this essay is about a character in a story, one natural pattern of organization is chronological order. The events in the story happened in chronological order — point by point on a time line — so she can use the same time line to arrange her paragraphs. And that's what she does, too. Point 1 happens first. Next comes point 2a. Then come the consequences, 2b. And so on, all the way down to the fourth paragraph.

There's also a textual pattern here. The paragraphs are arranged according to where they are located in the book. Point 1 happens first in chapter 1. Point 2a happens a few pages later. Point 2b is on the page after that. Point 3 is about twenty pages later. And so on, all the way down to the fourth paragraph, where things happen in later chapters.

Overlaid on top of those two patterns is a naturally occurring pattern of ranking by seriousness. Based on its consequences, the first thoughtless action is serious. The next is more serious. The third is most serious. The fourth paragraph doesn't really fit in the pattern, but that's okay. It's held in place by the chronological and textual patterns.

Finally, *within* the first three points, the evidence is organized by a cause-and-effect pattern. First Jane does something dumb. That's the cause. Then she bears the consequences. That's the effect.

Prioritizing the evidence first gave the student the ranking pattern. The chronological and textual patterns were just dumb luck — which happens a lot when you're writing about texts. It isn't always this easy, but you'll often find that organization is already built into your evidence.

Step 5: Write the Actual Topic Sentences

The final step in building a topic sentence outline is to write the topic sentences. Those sentences usually need to do three things:

1. Tell your readers what point the paragraph will present.

2. Connect the paragraph to your thesis or topic or another supporting idea within the body.

3. Let readers know how the paragraph fits into a pattern of organization.

I'll show you how our student writer does all three things in her topic sentences with my own comments in [brackets]:

1. **One early** [suggests chronological pattern] **example of this error in judgment** [connects to thesis — an example of the mistake] **comes from chapter 1** [suggests a textual pattern] **when Jane has a fight with her cousin, John Reed** [the evidence that this paragraph presents].

2a. **In spite of these fairly severe consequences** [refers to the last paragraph], **Jane makes the same basic mistake** [refers to the thesis — another example] **soon after her red-room experience** [suggests a chronological pattern] **by physically attacking her cousin** [the evidence that this paragraph will present].

2b. **This time,** [refers to previous paragraph] **the consequences** [suggests a cause-and-effect pattern, which is also chronological] **for Jane's mistake are more severe than a trip to the red-room or dinner by herself** [connects this paragraph by comparison to the first example].

3a. **Before Jane leaves Gateshead,** [suggests a chronological pattern] **she makes the same mistake** [refers to the thesis — one more example] **one last time** [suggests a chronological pattern] **by attacking her aunt directly** [the evidence that this paragraph will present].

3b. **The consequences** [suggests a cause-and-effect pattern, which is also chronological pattern] **for Jane's third mistake** [connects this paragraph to the previous one] **are the most severe** [connects this mistake to the other two by comparing the severity of the consequences.]

4. **The same basic mistake** [connects to the thesis] **continues** [suggests a chronological pattern] **throughout the entire first half of the novel** [suggests a textual pattern — also what this paragraph will present].

See how that works? It takes a little time to build a topic sentence outline, but when you do this one step at a time, it's not as difficult as it seems at first. It also makes the essay much easier to write, which will actually save you time in the long run.

Or Build a Topic Sentence Outline Afterward

Many professors require students to hand in a topic sentence outline with their rough drafts, but they're not idiots. They understand that many of their students create the topic sentence outline *after* they write the rough draft — not beforehand, like they are supposed to do — by looking at the paragraphs they just drafted and pulling out the topic sentences.

These student writers assume that the topic sentence outline is a useless exercise because — and this makes some sense — they have never needed to use one. They continue to write how they have always written, letting the words "flow" from their brains and hoping that the final product makes sense. They then write the topic sentence outline as a bit of busywork to keep their professor from preaching one more sermon about the practical and moral value of the topic sentence outline.

That sermon, by the way, goes something like this: You're not in high school anymore, student writer. This is not informal writing. These are formal papers, and formal papers must carefully present one main idea. It's hard to stick to one main idea when you plunge ahead into drafting. Once the creative process of drafting begins, your mind has a way of going where it wants to go — like a big, slobbering dog that pulls you by its leash off the sidewalk and into traffic. When you don't have an outline to help you stick to your main idea, it's easy to stray from your main idea.

That's why your professors ask you to create outlines first. It's for your sake, not theirs. But if you insist on ignoring your professor's thoughtful advice and drafting your essay without first creating an outline, creating a topic sentence outline afterward can still help you clean up problems in the draft. So fine. Go to each body paragraph, extract the one sentence that tells readers what to expect from the paragraph, and put that in your outline. You will quickly discover several valuable benefits for your labors.

First, if no topic sentence exists in a paragraph, your after-the-draft topic sentence outline points out this deficiency. As long as that paragraph is focused on one supporting idea, you can then create a topic sentence for it. That will make the paragraph more effective. You might also find that there's no topic sentence in a paragraph because the paragraph doesn't really have one main point to make. If that's what you discover, you can take a quiet moment to rethink the paragraph as a whole. Does the information belong in some other paragraph? Could you expand on one idea to make this a paragraph that does support your thesis? Do you need to cut this paragraph? Hard decisions, student writer, but that's the way we like it.

Second, this also gives you an opportunity to rewrite your topic sentences. Remember those three pieces of information that a good topic sentence provides:

1. Tells your readers what point the paragraph will present.

2. Connects the paragraph to your thesis or topic or another supporting idea within the body.

3. Lets readers know how the paragraph fits into a pattern of organization.

Do all of your topic sentences provide that information? They don't? Well, do something about that.

Finally, this kind of outline also helps you organize your paragraphs. It allows you to look at the body of the essay as a list of sentences on a single page, and that makes it much easier to identify patterns of organization or a complete absence of organization. It also makes it easier to see how to move paragraphs around to make them fit into a pattern.

An after-the-draft topic sentence outline is thus a good way to revise your rough draft while it's still pliable. Your professor and I still say that you're better off planning the body of your essay before you write it. However, if you find yourself stuck when it comes to creating a before-the-draft outline, it's not the worst thing in the world to draft the body of the essay first and then come back and revise it with a topic sentence outline. Just do it thoughtfully.

Organize Your Paragraphs

It's possible to write an effective short essay that has no organization other than an opening paragraph, followed by a body of explanation, followed by a closing paragraph. You could write a letter to the editor like that, or an answer on a midterm exam, or a humorous e-mail to a soon-to-be-former boyfriend who was hurt and offended by the way you playfully kicked his precious cat, Mr. Mouser. You really just nudged him a little with your foot. These bits of writing are too short to be very confusing. Readers can mentally assemble the details whether or not they're formally organized.

While you don't need to worry much about organization when your essay is short, you do need to worry about it the rest of the time. Longer papers provide more complex explanations and more detailed information. Without organization, readers have a hard time keeping track of these details and connecting them to your main idea. They forget things. Their minds start to wander. It's like shopping for groceries without a basket or a cart. You can only hold so many things in your arms before you start dropping them.

Organization provides a shopping cart for your readers. The better the organization, the more information they can carry in their cart-enhanced brains. It's not a matter of putting "first," "second," and "third" at the beginning of paragraphs. It's a matter of arranging the paragraphs within larger patterns so that your readers know why the first paragraph comes first, the second comes second, and so on. And what's remarkable about organization is that the more patterns you use, the easier the essay is to follow. We humans love harmony — all of us, even anarchists — so the more something is organized, the more sense it makes.

Chapter 2 introduced you to a few key patterns that tend to be fairly useful — **chronological**, **textual**, and **ranking**. You saw that earlier in this chapter, too. But you have many more patterns to choose from, and that's what we'll look at for the rest of this chapter.

Use Obvious Patterns First

The most effective patterns of organization tend to be the most obvious ones. What makes them obvious is that they are a natural part of the topic or the information that you are explaining. What makes them effective is that they're natural parts of your readers' lives, too.

When it's time to organize, then, the first thing to do is to take a long, hard look at your evidence. What are the obvious patterns within that evidence? Below are some of the patterns that you are likely to see when you study your evidence in this way.

Chronological

A chronological pattern is based on when specific events happen. This pattern helps you present illustrations from case studies, hypothetical situations, historical events, and predicted future events. The pattern might start from beginning to end or start at the end and work its way backward. Either way, you're still using time to organize the details of your illustration.

We've already had a pretty good look at this pattern in chapter 2, so I won't go on and on about it here. I'll just go on a little more about why this pattern is so obvious with the *Jane Eyre* essay. It's because the topic is a story. Stories are chronological. That's just how they work. Even when an author goes to great lengths to cut up a story and rearrange the pieces for us, that's just a puzzle that we solve by putting those pieces back in chronological order. So using time to organize an essay about a story like this is an obvious choice.

And because your readers are creatures of time and space, they understand how time works. It's how their own lives are organized — one minute after another, like it or not — so it's also an easy pattern for them to use for organizing the details of your essay in their own minds.

Textual

With a textual pattern, you use the structure of a text — which is probably your topic — to structure your essay. You write about what happens early in the text first, and then what happens in the middle next, and then what happens in the end last. You saw that in chapter 2 as well.

Because *Jane Eyre* is a book that breaks down into chapters and then into pages, an obvious way to organize an essay about this novel is to use the arrangement of the chapters as a pattern of organization for the essay. And again, your readers get that. Books are a part of their lives, so they understand that books are organized into chapters, that chapters are made of pages, and that pages are numbered from beginning to end, read from top to bottom, and so on. That past experience with books and other written works makes it easy for readers to follow a paper about a book — or a poem, or a short story, or a newspaper article.

A textual pattern is an obvious pattern to use when your essay responds to a text, but you can use it with films, theatrical productions, music, and more. You just treat that non-printed topic as if it were a book, broken down into parts that are broken down into smaller parts. You use the shape of that visual or aural "text" as the shape of your paper.

Spatial

A spatial — that is, space — pattern usually arranges your detailed information according to where it happened or is happening or will happen. And once again, this is an obvious pattern to use for most real-world topics because most real-world topics exist in the — wait for it — real world. Just like you and your readers, one would hope. In the same way that we understand time as a pattern, we understand location as a pattern. We know how it works. We see that with every step we take.

We could use that to write about Jane Eyre, too, because our title character does get around. She lives in five different homes in this novel, so if we were to write about how she eventually grows up and learns to keep her mouth shut, we could organize our essay according to where she lived in this journey of self-editing:

1. At Gateshead, she does not edit herself much at all.

2. At Lowood, she begins to stop sassing the teachers.

3. At Thornfield, she holds her tongue around most of her social betters.

4. At Moor House, she actually keeps a few secrets.

5. At Ferndean Manor, she begins to hide her thoughts from her readers.

This example uses actual locations as its framework, and it follows Jane as she travels from one house to the next. It also uses chronological order because Jane, like most people, could only be at one place at a time, but as you already know, using two patterns at once is not a problem.

Visual

Visual patterns are spatial patterns that are not linked to time. These patterns function in the same way that a camera lens works, moving from a wide view of a situation to a close-up view or vice versa. If you write about how Jane Eyre illustrates the vulnerability of the governess in nineteenth-century England, for example, you could organize the paper like this:

1. An overview of governesses in England

2. Jane's governess position at Thornfield

3. Jane and Rochester in Rochester's private chambers

Do you see how that's like a camera lens taking a broad view of the situation and then zooming in to take a closer — and then closer — view of Jane's vulnerability?

Components

This pattern divides the whole topic into all of its various parts and uses those components as a way to group detailed information into larger chunks that explain the idea as a whole. You can use this pattern with any topic because any topic can be divided into parts. And again, if you've been paying attention, you've probably noticed by now that just about everything in this world can be divided into parts, so it's another easy pattern for readers to follow. But you can't leave anything out. You have to take the whole topic, break it apart into parts, and then show your readers all of the parts, one by one.

In the middle of *Jane Eyre*, our main character is summoned back to Gateshead, where she started, to help her Aunt Reed die a horrible death that is made about three percent less horrible by her confession to Jane that she blocked Jane's rich uncle from contacting her. What a soap opera. Anyway, it's actually a telling moment in the book because we get to see Jane and the Reed children as grown-ups, so we can take a look at the paths they are taking into adulthood.

You could use this pattern to talk about the cousins as a group by looking at them one by one:

1. John Reed has drunk and gambled himself to death.

2. Eliza Reed is in the process of becoming a devoutly uncompassionate person — and someday a Mother Superior.

3. Georgiana Reed is still as pretty and shallow and dumb as ever.

4. Jane is compassionate, intelligent, virtuous, and — possibly — rich, rich, rich.

You may notice that although the component pattern provides a basic structure for the essay — which is fine on its own — this list also uses a chronological pattern to organize the components on the list. We move by birth order from oldest to youngest. That makes a good thing even better.

Or Use Logical Patterns

Sometimes information comes to you with built-in, obvious patterns. Sometimes it doesn't. And sometimes you'll find that the obvious patterns don't help you make your point very well. When that happens, you have to take a step back and develop a more sophisticated pattern that reflects your own thinking about the topic. That thinking is what makes these patterns logical. They reflect your judgment about what the information means.

Suppose, for example, that in looking at how all the Reed cousins have turned out as adults, you notice that the Reeds don't really measure up to poor, pitiful Jane anymore. That's not a super insightful idea, but it's okay. This is the first time you've read the novel, after all. If you were to write about that idea, you can use the components and chronological pattern you just saw to organize your essay. However, that means you don't talk about Jane until the end of the essay. It makes more sense to talk about her first as the standard by which all Reed cousins are measured.

If you reverse the chronological pattern and move from youngest to oldest, that puts Jane first, and that's better. However, to make your point even clearer, you can also organize those cousins by how close they come to measuring up to Jane. In that case, you'd be ranking them by their Janeliness:

1. Jane is the most Jane-like, obviously.

2. Eliza Reed is somewhat like Jane — in her intelligence, anyway — but her religion falls well short of Jane's virtue.

3. Georgiana Reed is only slightly like Jane in her emotional tenderness but otherwise far less virtuous or intelligent.

4. John Reed was a lout and never measured up to Jane in intelligence or emotions or virtue or anything, pour soul.

This is a logical pattern — a ranking — that depends on your judgment of these cousins. You have taken Jane as the standard and measured each of them. These aren't facts. These are your logical conclusions about what the facts mean. That's how logical patterns are formed — you form them by finding patterns of meaning in the evidence.

We'll look at some logical patterns in just a minute. But first, I need to point out — because it comes up all the time — that chronological is *not* a logical pattern, even though it has that "logical" part staring up at you from the page. Time is a naturally occurring pattern in this world. It's an obvious pattern because it's already built into a lot of evidence, and no thanks to you, either. It's not something you figured out. It's just there.

Ranking

When you rank a set of items — reasons, groups of evidence, examples, whatever else your paragraphs have to offer — you arrange those items in a most-to-least or least-to-most pattern. That's easy enough to do, but first you figure out most to least of *what*. What quality or characteristic will you use for your ranking?

That answer is fairly straightforward when you're ranking something tangible — cars, cities, dancing shoes, characters in Charlotte Brontë's epic novel, *Jane Eyre*. You just pick something that they all have in common — horsepower, population, cost, Janeliness — and rank them according to how much they have of that characteristic. And although it's a little less tangible, you can do the same basic thing with reasons, solutions, proposals, and other less tangible commodities. You focus on something they all have in common — effectiveness, importance, cost — and rank them by that characteristic.

On the previous page, you saw an example of ranking according to the characteristic of Janeliness. That's fine for that idea. If you were to argue that the Reed cousins were meaner than Jane, you could rank them according to the characteristic of meanness:

1. John Reed is inwardly and outwardly mean to everyone he knows, even his mother.

2. Eliza Reed is mean to many others but is quiet about it.

3. Georgiana Reed is not mean.

Or you could reverse the ranking if you wanted to build up to the meanest:

1. Not mean — Georgiana Reed

2. Mean — Eliza Reed

3. Very mean — John Reed

Ranking is a useful organization pattern with a lot of ideas. Even if you don't use it as your main pattern of organization, you're likely to use it to organized subsections within your paper.

Cause and Effect

This is a type of chronological pattern that depends on your logical inter-pretation about two chronological events. You are proposing that one event caused the other. That is not a fact. It's your interpretation of the facts, and that's what makes this a logical pattern. One of the questions about Jane Eyre as a child is whether she's the cause of her own problems. Our student writer from chapter 2 certainly thought so. And you saw that in her organi-zation of several paragraphs:

1. Cause: Jane mouths off to her aunt.

2. Effect: Aunt Reed sends Jane away from relative comfort.

3. Effect: Jane lives amid disease, loneliness, and poor instruction.

4. Effect: Aunt Reed blocks Jane's rich uncle from rescuing her.

That was that student's view of the facts. But another way of looking at the fact is that Jane spoke out because of how badly she was treated by the Reeds. So you could also use cause and effect to organize the evidence for that idea, but it would look a little different:

1. Cause: Aunt Reed never wanted Jane there.

2. Cause: The Reed kids treat Jane like an unwanted outsider.

3. Cause: Aunt Reed segregates Jane from her children.

4. Effect: Jane mouths off to her aunt.

Once again, you see overlapping patterns at work in both of these examples. First, you have the logical cause-and-effect pattern. Then you have chronological and textual patterns that organize the effects of the first example and the causes of the second one.

Problem and Solution

This is another logical pattern you can use whenever your focus is to propose a policy that will address whatever problem you have in mind. Prob-lem-and-solution essays almost always follow the same general pattern:

1. Identify the problem and its development.

2. Propose a solution and its effects, costs, and so on.

3. Consider alternative solutions and their effects, costs, and so on.

4. Conclude by presenting your solution as the best one for this problem.

This pattern tends to be chronological because your problem developed in the past, exists in the present, and — if you have your way — will change in the future. But you're not stuck with that. You could use other patterns like ranking to sort out and arrange the solutions and the effects of those solutions. However, the general chronological pattern will remain as the backbone of a problem-and-solution essay.

Comparison

A comparison pattern is useful when your essay focuses on two or more similar things — objects, ideas, people, words, *anything* — and your thesis is a conclusion that's based on a side-by-side examination of those similar things.

One interesting moment in *Jane Eyre* is when — spoiler alert! — Jane discovers that her significantly older fiancé, Rochester, already has a wife who is living a somewhat unfulfilling life in the attic. It's an obvious choice to compare Jane and Rochester's wife, Bertha, because they have Rochester in common as a mutual love interest. They are the two similar things.

So let's suppose that by examining these two characters closely, you conclude that Jane and Bertha have the same essential problem — a lack of self-determination — and that you see this playing out emotionally, physically, and socially. You have two main options for organizing your evidence for this idea — **alternating pattern** or **block pattern**. The alternating pattern groups the evidence by your points of comparison. The block pattern groups the evidence by the things that you're comparing.

With an alternating comparison, your organization looks like this:

1. Emotional self-determination

    a. Jane evidence

    b. Bertha evidence

    2. Physical self-determination

       a. Jane evidence

       b. Bertha evidence

    3. Social self-determination

       a. Jane evidence

       b. Bertha evidence

With the same basic information and a block pattern, the body of your essay might look like this:

    A. Jane lacks self-determination

       1. Emotional evidence

       2. Physical evidence

       3. Social evidence

    B. Bertha also lacks self-determination

       1. Emotional evidence

       2. Physical evidence

       3. Social evidence

It's a good idea to arrange your points of comparison according to another pattern whenever one is available. We don't have a very obvious one with this example, which suddenly makes me wonder about the value of this example, but there is still a type of ranking that could be used, moving from most personal to least personal contexts.

What matters more, though, is that you use a parallel structure with comparison. In the alternating pattern, for example, each of the points of comparison looks at Jane and then at Bertha. Bertha never comes first. In the block pattern, the points of comparison are presented in the same order for Jane as they are for Bertha. The parallel structure helps readers make a clearer comparison because the details are laid out in the same order.

Listing

Sometimes you have many smaller, equal points to make and can't figure out any meaningful pattern that would organize those details. Perhaps you have six or seven reasons to support a proposal or nine examples of some other idea in action. When that kind of abundance happens, and when all the evidence is weighted equally, then numbering each item might be enough of a framework for your readers.

We had an example of this in the first part of the chapter when our student writer was working on her topic sentence outline. She started by listing nine examples of Jane failing to self-edit. The reason she couldn't use listing, however, is that they were not equal in weight. Some were more serious than others. Some were more tangible than others. Some were more complex than others. Listing only makes sense when all the points are brief and roughly equal in importance.

So we'll turn to another text to illustrate this technique. Here's part of Mark Twain's somewhat snooty essay, "Fenimore Cooper's Literary Offenses":

> There are nineteen rules governing literary art in the domain of romantic fiction — some say twenty-two. In *Deerslayer*, Cooper violated eighteen of them. These eighteen require:
>
> 1. That a tale shall accomplish something and arrive somewhere. But the *Deerslayer* tale accomplishes nothing and arrives in air.
>
> 2. They require that the episodes in a tale shall be necessary parts of the tale, and shall help to develop it. But as the *Deerslayer* tale is not a tale, and accomplishes nothing and arrives nowhere, the episodes have no rightful place in the work, since there was nothing for them to develop.
>
> 3. They require that the personages in a tale shall be alive, except in the case of corpses, and that always the reader shall be able to tell the corpses from the others. But this detail has often been overlooked in the *Deerslayer* tale. . . .

And so on through the rest of the examples. This is sheer volume — so much nit-picking evidence that there seems to be no rebuttal to Twain's idea. Listing gives the impression that Twain could give examples all night long, which he probably could have.

I hesitate even telling you about listing because it's not *really* a pattern. It just looks like one. It's the same as saying "first," "second," and "third" when there's no actual pattern being used to make one thing first and another thing second. It's not a great idea almost all of the time. So, of course, as soon as my students see that listing is an option, they sing out, "Perfect! I'll organize my essay with listing. Problem solved!"

Problem *not* solved, student writer. Because listing only makes sense when you have a ton of relatively equal pieces of evidence to share. That doesn't happen very often — maybe once every twenty papers that you write. So be careful.

The Big Ideas

After you have used evidence to figure out your main idea, you can begin to plan the essay that explains your main idea. That largely means organizing the information and ideas that led you to your main idea. Here are the big ideas about how this works:

1. Topic sentence outlines before you draft: One great way to organize the body of your essay is with a topic sentence outline. But don't start by trying to write finished topic sentences. That's a tough road to walk. Instead, start with some easy preliminary steps and work your way up to topic sentences.

2. Topic sentence outlines after you draft: If you refuse to create an outline *before* you draft the essay, then use a topic sentence outline afterward. It will help you make sure that your body paragraphs are effective and organized, that your drafting didn't go sideways.

3. Organization: The best patterns for organization are obvious ones. These are patterns like time, location, and components that are a natural part of the evidence and the world we all live in. Readers understand those patterns easily. However, you have other options, too, and sometimes they are more effective.

Chapter 10
Explain Your Idea with Details

Because you've planned the body of your essay with a topic sentence outline — and you have, haven't you? — writing the rough draft is no longer a matter of figuring out, paragraph by paragraph, what comes next. Now it's a matter of sharing, paragraph by paragraph, the supporting sentences required by your topic sentence outline. That's a lot easier, and for most student writers, it's a huge relief from the stress of having to make things up as they go along.

Writing the rough draft is still hard work, however, so don't get carried away. You need to explain your idea with sufficient information, and it needs to be *detailed* information. Whenever you bring that outside information into your essay, you also need to give credit to its source. That's what we'll look at in this chapter. We're still only working on the body of your essay, by the way. Openings and closings will have to wait for the next chapter.

Define Important Words

The first thing to do in the body of your essay is to clarify what you mean by the idea your opening introduces. When you developed your writerly thesis statement for this essay, you replaced vague terms with more precise ones. Now that you're presenting your main idea to your readers, they need to know exactly what you mean, too. So it's a good idea to use the first paragraph in the body to define those key terms.

A definition is like a fence. Inside that fence is what you mean by that word. Outside that fence are all the other possible meanings that you — for this essay — are going to happily ignore. Suppose, for example, that your main idea is that fast food is bad food. "Fast food" and "bad food" can mean a lot of different things. Left undefined, they'd require miles of fence to contain all the possible meanings. So if by "fast food" you only mean meals prepared by national hamburger chains — or maybe just one hamburger chain — then you tell that to your readers so they don't get the wrong idea about what to expect inside your fast-food fence. "Bad food" requires an even larger fence for its possible meanings. So if by "bad food" you only mean "harmful to the workers who prepare it," then use that tiny little fence instead of "bad food" so that your readers won't wonder why all the other possible meanings of "bad food" aren't in your essay.

Your definitions of the key words should match the information you're going to present. If your information about fast food is limited to one national chain of restaurants, then define "fast food" to mean the food from that chain. If your information is focused on deep-fried foods, then define "fast food" as "anything cooked in a deep fryer." That's a pretty narrow definition of fast food, but if that's the nature of your information, then that's where you need to build your fence. It tells readers that the other definitions of "fast food" won't be part of your essay.

You can also define what's inside the fence of your definition by pointedly stating what's *not* inside the fence. You might suspect, for example, that "fast food" means hamburger chains to a lot of people. If that's not what you mean, then tell your readers to set aside that hamburger-chain definition. Negation can be used anytime, but it's particularly important when your key terms are commonly understood to mean something other than what you have in mind.

Examples also help to clarify your definitions. Whether they're hypothetical, personal, or historical, they show readers what your definition looks like in real life. If you define "fast food" as anything cooked in four minutes or less, you can then offer a list of possible examples — hamburgers, microwave popcorn, corn dogs, deep-fried pickles — that help readers see just how broad or narrow your definition's boundaries are. Examples are particularly effective when your key terms are abstract. If by "profane" you mean "showing contempt for sacred things," your abstract definition might still be hard for some readers to understand. If you give them an example of what this looks like — spitting on a church, for example — the definition becomes clearer.

Your essay satisfies its readers by living up to the expectations you give them when you first explain your idea. If they know exactly what you mean up front, then they also have a more realistic expectation of what information they should expect in the rest of the body. So the more clearly you define your idea, the better chance you have of fulfilling the expectations of your readers.

Use Summaries to Introduce or Interpret Information

A summary is a statement that compresses a lot of details into a smaller set of words. When you present the detailed information that explains and illustrates your main idea, you'll need to use summaries to tell your readers the meaning of those details.

For most paragraphs, you should use a topic sentence to summarize the detailed information that's presented by the supporting sentences in that paragraph. As the first sentence in a paragraph, a topic sentence tells readers what to expect, and the details in the paragraph then satisfy that expectation. If you end with a topic sentence, it summarizes the meaning of all the details that went before it. If you put a topic sentence in the middle of a paragraph, it's usually to show readers how the details before the topic sentence are related to the details that follow.

No matter where you place a topic sentence, the effect on your readers is about the same. It satisfies. They sit back and think, "Nice paragraph. I see what you mean." Careful readers will still be able to figure out the general idea or purpose of a paragraph without the use of a topic sentence, but a good topic sentence will tell them what *you* think the information means, and that's important, too.

A topic sentence also tells readers what aspect of the main idea you're going to focus on in that paragraph. If your topic sentence says that *Casablanca* is tediously predictable, for example, you've summarized a single quality about the movie. Readers will now expect the details of that paragraph to explain why the plot of the movie is easy to predict. Just as importantly, it also shows readers that you will *not* be looking at the many other characteristics of the movie — the dreary cinematography, the inept casting, the annoying way that Humphrey Bogart sucks on his teeth throughout the movie.

Although summaries are essential, they're never enough. If you only present a summary and leave out the detailed information, you're telling your readers, "Trust me." Some readers might trust you, but careful readers will not. A careful reader needs to see some or all of the detailed information you are summarizing in order to test the validity of your summary and, to a lesser extent, to measure your abilities as an interpreter of information.

At first glance, this seems kind of mean, doesn't it? Why can't people just trust you? Student writer, it's because you're human, and humans are screw-ups, even when they mean well. They cut corners. They get lazy. They exaggerate. They think the best of people even when they know they shouldn't. So while it might *look* mean for someone to expect you to back up your summary with detailed information, you could also say that the careful reader is helping you become a better writer — and person, possibly. There's some positive spin for you.

One other problem with relying on summaries, which is especially important for those of you who begin to whimper and mew when assigned a minimum length for an essay, is that summaries compress acres of detailed information into puny little hedgerows of words. Relying on summaries without including those acres of detailed information will leave you with too little to say.

Use Details to Defend Your Summaries

Details are small pieces of real-world information. They explain how things sound, feel, taste, smell, and look. They are the specific prices of items at a grocery store. They are the shouted insults, bloodied noses, and broken windows that together become a historical event. The actual wording of immigration laws, the actual number of killer bees counted by a biologist, the actual weight in milligrams of a really good banana split. Even if the details are made up — as with hypothetical situations — they must be connected to reality by particulars that your readers *might* see, hear, smell, and so on.

Details show readers what your summaries look like in the real world. Their primary work is to establish the objectivity of those summaries and your main idea. However, they also give readers mental images, something that readers can see for themselves with their imaginations. Those mental images are more powerful and interesting than the summaries. Readers love it when their imaginations kick into action.

Consider this summarizing sentence: "To keep a relationship healthy, you have to keep it new." That's not terrible as a summary, but left to itself, it's just your opinion — and who are you to tell your readers how to keep their relationships healthy? To make this idea understood and objective, you have to show readers what you mean with detailed information. Here's an example of how you might do this with a hypothetical situation:

> With someone you know very well, such as a long-term girlfriend, you might fall into the trap of thinking that there's nothing new for you to learn about her or for her to learn about you. Instead of asking her about her dreams, you ask her to pass the salt. Instead of sharing your fears and desires with her, you share the Metro section of the paper and maybe half of your bagel. Maybe. Gradually, a relationship that used to be full of surprises becomes full of routines and habits and long hours of watching *Masterpiece Theatre* in silence. It becomes static. It becomes your parents' marriage. But people are always changing — you know that because *you* are always changing — so no matter how well you think you know your long-term girlfriend, you'd be an idiot to think you've learned everything about her. You'd be a bigger idiot to treat the relationship like it was a toaster you paid for a long time ago. To keep a relationship healthy, you have to keep it new.

The details show your readers what you mean by "relationship" and "keep it new." They get the readers' imaginations going, too, because there are particulars here they can visualize. Most importantly, the details demonstrate that such a problem is possible in the real world, that you're not making this up out of thin air. That helps your readers take you and what you tell them more seriously.

The only unfortunate side effect of giving your readers the detailed information they require is that it takes time to do it right. Putting detailed information into words has a tendency to wear out student writers. After spending two or three hours assembling precise, detailed explanations, student writers often tire of their own writing and start to cut out details for fear of boring their readers.

Foolish student writers!

Yes, after you spend hours and hours working with detailed information, those details may grow dull by familiarity — for you. However, your readers will only spend ten minutes with this same set of details. For your readers, these details aren't boring at all. They show your readers that you've put some thought and research into your essay, that you have a sound basis for your answer to the question. Those details also give your readers something to assemble with their imaginations, too, and they like doing that.

If you don't believe me, try this little science experiment. Write your essay in advance, set it aside for two days, and then read it. The same details that wearied you two days ago will miraculously become convincing and engaging because the passage of time has changed you from a writer into a reader. On the writer side of the street, the details can wear you out. Familiarity breeds contempt. But on the reader side of the street, those same details are *great*. So hang in there. If you get tired, take a break. Go bowling. Shop online for a new toaster. Then come back and finish what you started.

It is *possible* to ruin an essay by filling it up with more illustration than your readers need. Some readers might start to suspect that you think they're dumb. In three decades of teaching, however, I've only seen that happen twice, maybe three times. It's not something for you to worry about, in other words. If you have room for more details, add them.

Use Details to Illustrate and Defend

In presenting your main idea, your first job is to illustrate it clearly so that readers understand what you mean. However, because your main idea is a reasonable *opinion*, you must also defend it by showing readers why you think it's a good idea. For that, you need evidence. Luckily, the information you found while educating yourself will allow you to both illustrate and defend your ideas. You just have to use the right information for each job.

With information that illustrates, the key quality is that it's detailed. It doesn't even have to be credible information when its job is only to explain and not to defend an idea. You could make up detailed hypothetical situations to illustrate your idea, and these would be as just as effective as actual situations because it's the details that readers need in order to understand how your idea works in the real world.

Information used as evidence has two main qualities. First, like illustration, it should be detailed. That way your readers can judge for themselves what the evidence means and whether your judgments are sound. If you use only a summary of evidence — that most Americans hate cats, for example — readers have to take your word for it. If you get into the details — in a recent Gallup poll, 341 out of 550 respondents reported that they "hate" cats, and another 86 said they "fundamentally disliked" cats — your readers can see for themselves that of course most Americans hate cats. This is why careful readers trust detailed information more than summarized information.

The second quality that makes evidence effective is objectivity. If an observation is objective, it can be measured or observed in some tangible way. The more objective the information is, the more useful it becomes as evidence because it shows your readers that the information is true in the real world, apart from individual perceptions and gut feelings.

This preference for the empirical doesn't mean that there is no spiritual reality or that your emotions aren't important. It doesn't mean that the many intangible elements in our lives — regret, for example, or an intense fear of clowns — are insignificant. Reliance upon objective information simply reflects our status as three-dimensional creatures. Those three dimensions are the common ground we share with other humans. Information that exists in three dimensions — numbers of salmon, words in a book, sworn courtroom testimony, and so on — can be observed or measured by anyone and thus becomes more reliable than internal or intangible information.

You have many types of information to use in the body of your essay. Some are better for illustrating and some are better for defending your main idea. What follows is a quick review of common types of information and their range of usefulness as illustration or evidence.

Personal Experience

The only reason I'm alive today is because I wasn't wearing a seat belt. If I had stayed in the car when it rolled, I would have been crushed to death.

Personal experience is a good way to engage your readers' imaginations because readers like stories. When it's detailed, a personal experience works well to illustrate an idea. However, personal experience is rarely effective for defending an idea because its scope is limited to you and because we all can so easily misunderstand our own experiences. Careful readers are rightly suspicious when personal experience is the basis for an entire essay. The example above is engaging enough as an opening illustration, but it would only serve as evidence for a very narrow idea — "seat belts don't *always* save lives."

Personal Observation

Some people smoke a couple packs of cigarettes a day and still live to a ripe old age. My great-aunt Marjorie was a chain-smoker and lived to be ninety-four. She never had health problems in all her years, and she would still be alive today if not for an unfortunate chainsaw accident.

Like personal experience, personal observation is useful primarily as a type of illustration that connects well with your readers. As evidence, it usually won't prove much of anything because we are rarely able to observe more than a narrow set of information and because we lack the training to judge the significance of that information.

Reference Information

Aristotle was a Greek philosopher. His writings create a comprehensive system of Western philosophy, including treatises on the topics of morality, aesthetics, logic, science, politics, cats, and metaphysics.

Except in the case of defining key terms, the information you find in reference works probably won't and shouldn't find a home in your essay. As you found earlier in the writing process, reference works are great for getting acquainted with a topic. They summarize broad bands of information so that you can get to know a topic quickly, and they often point you toward more detailed sources of information. However, they give you little detailed information. It's mostly summary. Because it's not detailed, the information from reference works won't be very effective as illustration or evidence. These reference works are still important, but their main job is to help you get to know your topic, not to provide the sort of evidence you need to share your ideas with others.

Professional Opinion or Observation

Chief Dye of the Chickawack Fire Department says that squirrels are second only to cigarettes as the source of home fires. According to Dye, squirrels chew the electrical wiring in attics, electrocuting themselves and bursting into dangerous, squirrel-shaped flames.

Professional observation is more credible than personal observation because the professional draws upon a broader range of training and experience than the average person. Even without scientific training, the firsthand experience and continuing education of the professional leads to more reliable observations and judgments. If professional observation is detailed, it can be good as illustration. It can be convincing evidence, too.

The key to using this type of information to defend an idea is making sure your professional is qualified to make observations about that subject. If the professional strays from her or his area of expertise, the value of that opinion quickly diminishes. That's like when an actor in a commercial tells you, "I'm not a doctor, but I play one on TV" — and then prescribes a pill for you. In the same way, a preacher's ideas about politics or a professional basketball player's ideas about religion shouldn't be taken more seriously than anyone else's personal observations and opinions.

Serious Popular Information

Bolivia has had 126 governments in 125 years of existence. More than 100 of these governments have been established by military coups like the one that took place last Tuesday when the leader of the Bolivian Navy took control of the government and immediately announced plans to attack Chile to gain access to the Pacific Ocean.

Serious popular information comes from newspapers, textbooks, magazines, and websites that are written for an educated but general audience. In many cases, these sources are written by scholars in the language of normal, non-nerdy people. In other cases, they are the work of professional writers who either discover the information themselves or translate the work of scholars into the language of normal, non-nerdy people.

The information from these sources is usually great for illustration because it makes complex ideas easier for normal people like your readers to understand. It's also useful as evidence when the topic is a news item or current issue. With those current topics, newspapers and magazines and news websites tend to provide the most reliable information.

For topics other than current events, however, you usually need to dig deeper into the topic to see if your serious popular information is accurate. With popular magazine and website articles, that means looking at the details of scholarly information to see if the professional writers have presented those ideas accurately. After you've done that, you don't really need the information from the magazine or website. You can use the more credible scholarly information instead.

Scholarly Information

The five-legged male Agalychnis callidryas *in Group A were 38% less likely to produce tremulations during breeding rituals than were the four-legged male* Agalychnis callidryas *of Group B. However, the attraction of four-legged females to the males of Group A was 13% higher than to the males of Group B. This suggests that Jabin (2014) may be correct in her theory that the five-legged* Agalychnis callidryas *don't need tremulation because the mutation itself attracts breeding partners who are curious to see what it's like to be with a five-legged mate.*

Scientific information is gathered and analyzed by people who, like other professionals, work with a certain body of knowledge all day long, year after year. However, these people have also been trained in standardized methods for developing and testing information and ideas. This training creates a level of quality control. Working within a scientific discipline also means that these professionals must publish their findings to their peers for review and testing. The publication process provides yet another layer of quality control because academic peers will gladly cut each other's throats over the slightest mistake.

There is still plenty of room for faulty, incomplete, or manipulated scientific information. Some scientists have made up study results to secure future grants and impress their friends. It also happens that a rogue government will sometimes edit the science in its agencies' reports for the sake of political goals. However, the scientific systems come with safeguards that clean up and remove that kind of junk — eventually.

Besides being more credible, scholarly information is usually more detailed than other sources of information. Scholars have to show their work to their peers, and that means showing them the detailed information upon which their ideas are founded. Those objective details — and the credible interpretations of scholars — are good types of evidence to use in your own essay.

As good as scholarly information is for defending ideas, it doesn't do well illustrating them. Not at all. Scholarly work is written in the professional language of professional scholars, people who are so deeply immersed in their disciplines that they rarely see the sun, much less speak in the language of normal people. Unless your audience is made up of professional scholars, you'll need to decode the scholarly information for the illustrations to make any sense. For most audiences, similar information from serious popular sources will be more effective as illustration.

Textual Information

Like you need another example of textual information.

When your topic is a text — a song, poem, play, essay, film, or classic Gothic romance about a young girl's rise from loud-mouthed poverty to demure prosperity — the best illustration and evidence for your essay is information from the text itself. You can use historical information or scholarly opinion about the text, but even that should mostly be used to explain the meaning of the textual information. It's best to rely on the text itself as the main source of your evidence. The more detailed that information is, the more effective it becomes as evidence because it shows readers that your ideas really are based on the text itself.

Give Credit to Your Sources of Information

Academic honesty and good manners require that whenever you use ideas or information from sources outside your own experience or observation, you must tell your readers where the information came from. That includes actual words, ideas, stories, summarized information, paraphrased descriptions — *anything.*

If you don't give credit to your sources, you're guilty of **plagiarism.** Unfortunately, "plagiarism" is just another vague English-teacher term for most student writers. It sounds like a mild medical condition, a foot rash or inflammation of the elbow. You got plagiarism? No big deal. Put some ice on it. Take an aspirin.

That's why I prefer to use a different word for plagiarism. I call it *stealing.* If you don't give credit to the sources of your information and ideas, you are a thief. You're taking the credit that belongs to another writer and giving it to yourself. Imagine how you'd feel about the person who breaks into your ancient Honda Civic and steals the car stereo that is worth more than the car itself? That's how you should feel about yourself when you don't give credit to others. You should feel like a jerk. You shouldn't feel okay about it.

The first step in giving credit to your sources is the *decision* to give credit to your sources. This is a choice you have to make for yourself. For that, you're on your own, just you and your conscience. If you and your conscience decide to not give credit, however, then you and your conscience might soon be assisted by the Dean of Students and his or her conscience. Because even if you feel okay about it, stealing words and ideas remains a serious offense at college, as the Dean of Students will explain in detail.

The second step is learning *how* to give credit to others. There's a lot of popular misinformation and plain old folklore out there about when you do or do not need to give credit to others, so do your best to get forget any ideas you already have about how this works. I don't mean any offense to you or your education to this point, but those ideas are probably wrong. Instead, pay close attention to the guidelines that follow — and then follow them, of course.

Give Credit When You Paraphrase or Summarize

We'll start with the biggest problem out there.

Contrary to popular belief, you can't just "put it into your own words" and call it good. Putting someone else's ideas or information into your own words doesn't make the ideas things that you thought of or the information something that you gathered. It only makes it look like you deserve all the credit — which is plagiarism. So whenever you use someone else's ideas or information in your essay — whether you quote it directly or rephrase it — you must tell your readers who did the original work that you have summarized.

As you write your own papers, you will likely summarize and paraphrase most of the information you use. Direct quotations should only be used when the original source is particularly important or states something exceptionally well. You just have to make sure that the readers can tell which ideas or information are coming from you and which are coming from some other source. Here's how it looks in practice:

> According to Kay Colantino's letter to the *Itemizer-Observer*, the corn dogs at the Texaco Food Mart are always less than four days old, and the burritos are always less than two days old.

> Chickawack Community College's Assistant to the Associate Dean of Instruction, Dr. Robert LeRoy, Ed. D., denies that boring lectures are torture because there's no sleep deprivation involved.

At first, it might seem a little cumbersome to do this properly — especially if you are using a lot of information from a lot of sources — but that's okay. It's a little cumbersome to do almost anything properly, especially when other people are involved. Cumbersome is better than lonely.

When Give Credit When You Borrow Actual Words

Sometimes the actual language of a source is particularly good at explaining something. Sometimes the exact phrasing of a text — such as the First Amendment of the United States Constitution — needs to be considered directly. In those cases, you can borrow the exact wording of language from your source, but you have to make sure it's clear which words are your own and which belong to the outside source. You do that with direct quotations, like this:

> In a recent letter to the *Itemizer-Observer*, Kay Colantino writes, "You people need to stop looking down your noses at Food Mart dining. At my gas station, the corn dogs are never more than three days old, and the burritos are updated *daily*."

> Regarding the use of torture at the community college, Chickawack Community College's Assistant to the Associate Dean of Instruction, Dr. Robert LeRoy, Ed. D., said that a boring lecture couldn't be considered torture because it "induces rather than deprives a student of sleep."

With shorter quotations like these, you weave the borrowed words into your own paragraphs. The first set of quotation marks shows readers the beginning of the borrowed words, and the second set shows them where the borrowing ends. With longer direct quotations, you use formatting to show readers that these words are borrowed. You saw examples of this with the *Jane Eyre* essay in chapter 2. When the student writer needed to quote a longer passage from the novel, she indented the left margin so that it was visually set apart from her own words.

Student writers will sometimes feel satisfied with putting quotation marks around borrowed words, like this:

> Many people think she's a hair fanatic. "Her hair makes you think she's hiding drugs in there, or perhaps a small animal. It's beyond big." It might be wrong to judge someone by how she does her hair, but hair is an important part of the impression a person gives.

The quotation marks are a start because they tell readers that these exact words came from someone other than yourself, but if you don't provide the specific source of those words, the original author hasn't received the credit that's due. It's also distracting. Your readers stop reading your paragraph and start wondering who the author is and where you found the quotation. You must instead identify the source directly, like this:

> Many people think she's a hair fanatic. In a recent *New Yorker* article, fashion critic Syd Darby writes, "Her hair makes you think she's hiding drugs in there, or perhaps a small animal. It's beyond big." It might be wrong to judge someone by how she does her hair, but hair is an important part of the impression a person gives.

Give Credit Precisely

You have to give credit to sources each time you use their information. It's not enough to introduce a source once and then let your readers guess which information came from the source and which came from you. You need to give credit *wherever* credit is due, too. Otherwise, it's not clear which parts belong to you and which belong to others. Here's how that looks in practice:

> Another threat to sea lions is their increasing addiction to high-grade marijuana. In the journal *Science*, J. Ballard provides evidence that bundles of marijuana jettisoned by smugglers have become a favorite meal for sea lions. The *San Diego Union-Tribune* reported that the annual number of reports of stoned sea lions has risen five-fold over the past ten years. This may seem harmless enough, a victimless crime, but a recent study by the Oregon Department of Fish and Wildlife suggests just the opposite. The increasing number of sea lions with "the munchies" has been connected to depleted steelhead runs, the harassment of heavily armed fishing fleets, and the consumption of poisonous three-legged starfish, which according to ranger Jill Rupert, "kind of look like Doritos." Together, these increased hazards have put sea lions at a much greater risk of extinction.

If most but not all of the information in a paragraph comes from a single outside source, your task is a little easier. But you must still clearly distinguish which material comes from you and which does not. This means moving through your paragraph sentence by sentence to show your readers who gets credit for what. You don't need to introduce the single source multiple times, but you do need to refer to it as needed:

> This past November, the *Kansas City Star* reported that beef simply does not taste as good as it used to. According to their exposé, "The Beef with Beef," reporter Van Stavern found that beef, once the king of meats, now regularly loses in taste tests to pork, chicken, and halibut. Stavern also found it mattered little whether the beef in question was cubed, ground, or jerked. This seems hard to believe, but when given this same test, my football-playing, gun-toting brothers all agreed that they preferred a lightly marinated chicken leg to a delicious cheeseburger. This raised an important question for me: Is the quality of the meat changing, or are our tastes changing? The *Star* exposé doesn't answer that question, but this essay will.

Another error to avoid is referring to "studies" as the source of information without identifying the alleged studies by title or authors. Sometimes the "studies" are made up by dishonest student writers who suppose that writing professors won't be able to recognize fake information. Little do they know, we sometimes can. More often, however, this vagueness comes from basically honest student writers who wrote down the information but not the website where they found it. They hope "studies" is sufficient. It's not.

When this failure of memory occurs — and it occurs all the time — you're faced with three options. One is to use the information without giving credit to its forgotten source. This is the easy thing to do, but it's also lazy and unprofessional. And it's *plagiarism* — the bleeding ulcer of academic disorders! The second option is to *not* use the sourceless information. That's ethical, which is good, but it also weakens your essay. A third option is to track down the actual source of the information so you can give it proper credit. This is the best way to solve this problem, even though it takes time and self-discipline. And even better, of course, would be to avoid the problem altogether by taking better notes as you educate yourself about your topic.

Give Credit Before You Use the Information

You should give credit to a source before you offer its information. If you present the information to readers and follow that with a statement of where it came from, you've given credit where credit is due, but you've also given your readers an unnecessary second or two of confusion.

Consider these two examples:

> Used coffee grounds contain traces of ammonia and tannic acid and should never be eaten, even as part of a nationally advertised diet plan. That's according to the Surgeon General Crawford.

> According to the Surgeon General Crawford, used coffee grounds contain traces of ammonia and tannic acid and should never be eaten, even as part of a nationally advertised diet plan.

Both examples say where the borrowed information came from, but the second does so without puzzling readers at any point. Formal documentation systems often allow you to cite your sources immediately after you use their information, so that's fine. However, even with formal documentation, your essay will tend to be more readable if you use the name of the author to introduce that information.

With Informal Papers, Give Credit with Attribution

In all of the examples above, you saw examples of **attribution**. This is an informal way to give credit to your sources by mentioning a few key pieces of information — often the author, title, and publication — in the body of the essay. That information connects your quotation or idea or bit of information to a specific source. It also provides your readers with enough information to allow them to find that source for themselves in case they want to learn more or check to see if you are being honest.

Attribution is a common practice in journalism, where it lives within a fairly complex set of guidelines and standards that we won't get into. For a journalist, it's sometimes okay to attribute information vaguely — "according to high-level sources" — in order to protect the source of that information from retribution. However, even for journalists, it's only okay when you really do have actual sources to protect. You don't have any high-level sources to quote, student writer, so your attributions must always be precise.

Attribution is a good starting point for giving credit to your sources, so it's often used with reflection papers and other informal assignments. In addition to the principles you've just read about, effective attribution also requires you to know how to punctuate direct and indirect quotations. If you don't know how to do that, spend some time with your handbook of English grammar and study the rules for quotation marks. They aren't *that* complicated.

With Formal Papers, Give Credit with Formal Documentation

With most academic papers, you will need to give credit to your sources with a system of formal documentation. You've probably run into formal documentation before now. Writers in the humanities — including your writing professors — tend to use a formal documentation system developed by the Modern Language Association (MLA). The MLA system requires you to mention the author and page number whenever you use information in your essay, like this:

> In *Call Me Herman*, Melville writes that *Moby-Dick* was never meant to be taken seriously (231).

> *Moby-Dick* was not intended as a philosophical treatise in the form of a whaling novel but "a series of hilarious hijinks intended just for laughs" (Slemenda 301).

At the end of the essay or term paper, the MLA system asks you to provide a full set of bibliographic information. Here's what works cited entries look like:

> Melville, Herman. *Call Me Herman: The Official Autobiography.* Boston: Owl Press, 1842.

> Slemenda, Steve. "Is Melville to Be Trusted?" *Journal of Whaling Studies* 39 (2003): 295-308.

This list of works cited allows precocious readers to find and read your sources. The last name and page number in the body of your paper sends your readers to the correct listing on the works cited page. They can then use that information to find the source and read it for themselves.

There are several other documentation systems out there. Many writers in the social sciences use a system developed by the American Psychological

Association (APA). This system requires you to cite the author and date of publication when you use information from a source. The rest of the source information goes into a bibliography at the end of the essay. Some science papers put a numbered list of sources at the end of the paper and then cite just the corresponding source number within the body.

All these systems have two things in common. First, they all cite sources briefly in the body of the paper and then provide full bibliographic information elsewhere — usually at the end of the paper. Second, the details about exactly how to do this are mind-numbingly complex. There's a different way to cite every slightly different type of source — books with one author, books with two authors, books in translation, websites, interviews, newspaper articles, articles retrieved from a database, articles read while on a train to Boston, and so on. To make matters worse, those rules change every few years when the scholars get together to collectively change their minds.

Formal documentation is a great thing, and it's great for the same basic reasons that formal writing is great. It provides a common set of rules for all students and scholars within a group of disciplines. Everyone knows what to expect, and when every paper meets those expectations, the only difference between one paper and another is the quality of ideas. That's how it should be — especially with college papers. You want your ideas to be seen and taken seriously, and you want everything else — formatting, sentence grammar, documentation — to be more or less invisible to your readers.

Even so, learning how to use formal documentation will take a day or two. So take a deep breath and then find a good reference guide. For all of these systems, one option is to buy the guidebook that's published by a particular scholarly organization. Most college handbooks also come with abbreviated versions of the guides that are still sufficient. If you have a handbook already, that's probably enough. And you can find what you need online for free at many academic websites, such as Purdue University's Online Writing Lab.

What you *shouldn't* do is try to memorize all those rules. That's too much. You'll start having dreams about punctuation and indentation, which is just weird, even for English majors. Just find a handbook that you like, and then practice using it. That's plenty.

The Big Ideas

The big ideas for this chapter boil down to one big idea — explain yourself in detail. What gets more complicated is how exactly to do that. Here are the main points about how to do that:

1. Define the important words: You and your readers both need to understand what exactly your paper will explain — and what it won't explain — so do this early in the body of the essay.

2. Use summaries sparingly: You need summaries to introduce details and explain what they prove. Topic sentences are a good example. However, if you rely on summaries, you end up hiding your evidence from your readers, and careful readers won't like that.

3. Rely on detailed information to illustrate and defend: Give your readers the evidence that led you to your main idea in the first place. Use detailed information to illustrate. Use detailed and credible information to defend.

4. Don't wimp out on details: You, the writer, will get tired of your detailed information before your readers do. Don't let that fatigue stop you from giving your readers what they crave. If you get tired of presenting all that detailed information, take a break and then keep going.

5. Always give credit to your sources: Always. Whether you quote, summarize, or paraphrase information, you must always give credit to the sources of that information. It shows your readers which ideas are yours and which come from others. Failure to do this is called plagiarism — a type of theft.

6. Give credit to your sources appropriately: With informal papers, use attribution to give credit to sources. With formal papers, use the type of formal documentation that is appropriate for that academic discipline.

Chapter 11
Guide Your Readers

Chapter 2 gave you a decent preview of how to guide your readers with the *Jane Eyre* essay that continues to haunt this book. Our student writer gave her readers an opening that told them what to expect for the body. In the body, she gave them topic sentences and transitions to help them work their way through the body paragraphs without getting lost. In the closing, she restated the main points from the body and returned to the main idea about Jane's biggest mistake. It was not bad work. You could do worse things than follow her example.

But here's the thing. That kind of guidance doesn't happen unless you *make* it happen. That means going back to the essay you just drafted and putting it there.

Why isn't it already there? Because you, student writer, didn't need to be guided through your own essay. When you look at what you've written, you see a paper that makes perfect sense. You see how your information defends your main idea. You see how the paragraphs fit together. You certainly don't need some closing paragraph to summarize the information you put into the body. Duh. It's in the body. And if anything *is* missing on the page, your brain fills in that missing piece so that you won't feel bad about screwing up. Your brain loves you. It still accepts you even if huge chunks of information remain nestled in your brain instead of written into your essay.

Your readers, having no direct access to your brain, only see the words that you actually use in the essay. If you leave gaps in your explanations, even small ones, your readers stumble. And even if you present all the information clearly, your readers still won't be as familiar with your idea and information as you are. From their perspective, the main idea might still be hard to figure out. All that detailed information, even if it is organized, might still appear disorganized or disconnected from a main idea.

Your readers aren't stupid. They just aren't you. For them, this is the first and probably only time they will see your essay. So they need some help from you. You have to make your main idea unavoidably clear in the opening. You have to point out the organization in the body with fairly obvious transitions. Okay, you tell them, here comes the *second* of my four examples. Okay, now you get the *third* of my four examples. It's like feeding a little kid. Open wide — here comes the choo-choo train! When it's time to wrap things up, you have to give your readers a closing that reminds them about the information they just read — even though *they just read it*, for crying out loud. And then you have to remind them, one more time, about your main idea.

> **"Your readers aren't stupid. They just aren't you. For them, this is the first and probably only time they will see your essay. So they need some help from you."**

You didn't have to worry about this when you were writing short, informal papers for a living. All you had to do in those olden times was bond with your readers by chatting them up as you explained things. But I hope you understand by now that formal writing doesn't work like that. It stays focused on its topic, not you and your readers. For that, you need more formal techniques. And that's what this chapter will give you.

Use Topic Sentences

A great way to guide your readers through the body of the essay is with topic sentences. You've seen how they tell readers what to expect from a paragraph. That's part of it. But you can also use topic sentences to show readers how paragraphs help explain the main idea. Here's a topic sentence for you:

Hydroelectricity does a lot of damage to the environment.

That's fine for introducing the main point of the paragraph. You read that, and you know what to expect from the paragraph — the environmental downside of hydroelectric power. But your topic sentence has so much more potential than this. It's like you at age fifteen, practically an adult but not trusted with the keys to the family car. Give your topic sentence more responsibility. Use it to show your readers how this sentence helps to explain your main idea about electric cars:

> Another reason that electric cars are not as "eco-friendly" as the automobile industry claims is that even the supposedly clean hydroelectricity does a lot of damage to the environment.

Well done, student writer. This topic sentence now shows readers what to expect from this paragraph — hydroelectricity's environmental damage — and also that this is a reason in support of the main idea about electric cars.

You can also use a topic sentence to show the relationship of one paragraph to another:

> Generating electricity with dams is bad for the environment, but generating electricity with coal-fired power plants is worse.

This topic sentence connects the current paragraph to the former one with the words "bad" and "worse." This is another reason why electricity — and the cars that love it — is not necessarily "eco-friendly." The relationship between paragraphs is a relationship of degree. It is a stronger reason because it will talk about greater harm. The second half of the sentence tells us to expect the supporting sentences to talk about coal-fired power plants.

You can also use topic sentences to show readers organization:

> However, generating electricity with nuclear fission does the worst damage to the environment.

The word "worst" — combined with "bad" and "worse" from the previous topic sentences — shows readers that you're using ranking to organize these body paragraphs. And you could do about the same thing by slipping other little transitional words into your topic sentences:

> In the early 1900s, coal-fired power plants were seen as clean and efficient sources of electricity, but the air pollution they create has killed lakes and rivers, ruined the air we breathe, and contributed to global warming.

In the 1930s, hydroelectricity was the clean answer to power generation, but now we know that dams have done irreparable harm to fish runs and weakened the health of the world's rivers.

In the 1970s, nuclear power was widely heralded as the solution to the world's energy needs, but the radioactive waste from these power plants has contaminated air, water, and soil — and that contamination will last for tens of thousands of years.

You can see where this is going. Clearly, solar power will turn out to be a huge disaster, too. We just haven't figured it out yet. Anyway, those date references in the topic sentences show us that the paragraphs in the body are organized with a chronological pattern.

So the first way to use topic sentences to guide your readers is to make sure your body paragraphs have them. So do that. Read the body and check to see that every paragraph has a topic sentence. You may find, to your horror, that some of your paragraphs don't. "What the — ?" you will say. Don't finish that sentence, horrified student writer. Instead, add the topic sentence and move on. You can then expand and rephrase those topic sentences so that they connect directly to your main idea, connect to other paragraphs, and point out the patterns of organization that you are hopefully following.

Use Transitions

Transitions — whether they are sentences, phrases, or individual words — help readers see how the parts of your essay fit together. You saw that in the topic sentences. They might connect two or three items, or they might point out the organization of the whole body.

Transitional sentences are usually found at the beginning and end of subsections within the essay. They might be topic sentences, or they might act like topic sentences for multi-paragraph sections of the essay. At a pivotal point in the body, you could even use a transitional paragraph to explain how the paragraphs that follow are related to the paragraphs before. Here's a transitional topic sentence:

> Now that we understand the chemical makeup of this seemingly benign substance, we can appreciate the true horror of addiction to high-fructose corn syrup.

This transitional sentence isn't a topic sentence. It's a bridge between the previous paragraphs, which explained the chemical makeup of high-fructose corn syrup, and the paragraphs we're about to read, which will look at the horror of addiction. You could put it at the start of the sentence and then follow with a topic sentence for that paragraph. You could also turn it into a very short paragraph between the two blocks of paragraphs it connects. Very short paragraphs like that tend to draw attention to themselves, so you don't want to use them unless they are worthy of that attention. In this case, it is.

Here are some other transitional sentences from the same, depressing essay, that could be used as either as topic sentences or the closing sentences of paragraphs that look ahead to the next one:

> So much for the chemical makeup — what about the effects of these chemicals on the user?

> Dehydration is only the first and least consequential effect, but even more troubling is the rapid rise in heart rate.

> As if these effects weren't bad enough, high-fructose corn syrup also leads to dangerous levels of hyperactivity that turn the "syrup-sucker" into a human whirligig.

> The worst effect, however, is the drawn-out depression that follows the abuse of high-fructose corn syrup, a depression that grows deeper and more difficult to escape with each round of syrup-sucking.

> With effects this severe, why are kids today turning from traditional recreational drugs to high-fructose corn syrup?

These sentences might seem a little obvious when pulled out of paragraphs and listed like this. That's okay. Collectively, these sentences help readers see a cause-and-effect and a ranking pattern of least to most harmful within the body of the essay. The repetition of the key term "syrup-sucking" also reminds readers, again and again, that this is the topic of the essay. That's exactly what your distracted readers need in order to fit together the pieces of your essay.

Transitional phrases and words work like transitional sentences, but they do so within sentences instead of standing on their own. They are easy and effective additions to topic sentences, but mostly you will use them to guide readers through the supporting sentences of a paragraph, like this:

> For a relationship to grow, you have to grow. You have to be willing to admit your mistakes and stop making them. **For example**, you might admit that **in the past** you were petty about splitting expenses exactly down the middle. You shouldn't have asked her to pay for half of a beer from which she only took a sip. **In the future**, you won't do that. **For another example**, you also admit that **in the past,** you were perhaps a little harsh in your comments about her appearance. You didn't need to ask if she was retaining water or just putting on weight. **In the future**, you won't make those comments, even if you're seriously wondering. **In the future**, you'll be kind and supportive. We all make mistakes, but that's not a very good excuse to keep making them.

These transitions connect supporting sentences to the topic sentence ("for example") and point out the organization ("in the past," "in the future"). Even when they seem to draw attention to themselves — as with the repetition of "in the future" and "in the past" — they're actually drawing attention to the organization and the main point, making it easier to see.

It's hard to overdo transitions. It's like the detailed information phenomenon. A lot of detailed information might bore you as the writer, but your readers thrive on it. In the same way, a lot of transitions may seem awkward and way too obvious for you as the writer. You don't need them any more than you'd need a dozen signs telling you how to get to your own house. But it's different for your readers. They need those signs. They've never been to your house. The more you can point out the way, the better.

Write Engaging but Obvious Openings

Once the body of your essay is complete, it's time to write the opening and closing. You learned to write opening paragraphs from your old friend, the five-paragraph trainer-essay. For that opening, you used some kind of catchy hook to introduce the topic:

> According to Webster, a "catastrophe" is "something that is catastrophic." That certainly describes my recent trip to Iowa.

And you followed it with your thesis statement:

> One should never vacation in Iowa because of the heat, the humidity, and the profuse sweating.

However, as you were told in chapter 2, that kind of opening is no longer adequate for your formal papers.

With formal writing, your opening doesn't try to hook readers. It only has one job to do, and that's to tell your readers exactly and obviously what they can expect from the paper. These readers come to your formal writing because they have to as professors, researchers, judges, scholarship committees, and so on, so your opening must show them that your paper is what they're looking for — that your essay matches the assignment, that your research paper focuses on a question that interests them as researchers, that your letter is about the same traffic ticket that they must judge, that your scholarship essay responds directly to their assigned topic.

At the same time, formal readers are people, too, and people like to use their imaginations. They like to feel curiosity working its magic within them. So as long as your opening clearly tells your readers what to expect from the paper, you can hook them *a little*. You just have to be subtle about how you do that.

We'll look at a few techniques you can use to show your readers what to expect and, quietly, engage their interest.

The Big Picture

Readers usually enjoy seeing the big picture before you zoom in to focus on that topic and present your main idea about it. Providing some context shows your readers that your topic is part of something larger, and that you're aware of this. It acknowledges the limitations of your essay, too, which is a good thing. It shows readers that you're only going to concentrate on one part of the big picture — and that you're doing this intentionally, not accidentally. Here's an example:

> The two-party political system has been part of the American scene since before there was a true sense of what "the American scene" was. It hasn't always been Republicans and Democrats, of course, but it has always been two main parties. Whenever a third party has arisen for one reason or another — the Bull Moose Party of Teddy Roosevelt's time or the Republican Party of the mid-1800s — the third party either gained enough power to displace one of the previous major parties or it faded away to become one more footnote in American history. With so many problems present in our current political mess, it's no wonder that reform parties are making headway in their efforts to enter this political system. However, the question remains whether or not today's minor parties will survive more than a few years.

In this opening, the writer presents the bigger picture of two-party politics in America and then zooms in to focus on whether a modern third party could make it in the American political system. If you have an interest in politics, or if you're surprised to learn that Republicans weren't there at the beginning, this might make you curious to read more.

You'll notice that you don't get a thesis statement with this opening. That's kind of strange, isn't it? The writer gives us a clear expectation of what the thesis will be — an answer to this question about third parties — but he doesn't state that answer. For that, you have to keep reading. It's a daring move, student writer, but unless your professor explicitly states that your opening must have a thesis statement, it's enough to introduce the topic, the focus, and what we can expect for the thesis.

Anecdotes

An anecdote is a brief story that uses a personal experience, hypothetical situation, historical incident, or other event to introduce the topic. It doesn't really matter whether you use real-life anecdotes or invented ones, either. Stories are stories, and people love stories. You can also start with just half of an anecdote and save the other half for your closing. Here's an example of an opening anecdote:

> When he was twenty-two, Daniel Couch shot himself. It happened while he was cleaning out his uncle's trailer. His uncle had been using the drawer of his bedside table for an ashtray, and when Daniel dumped the cigarette

butts into the garbage can, he found that his uncle had also been using the drawer as a gun locker. His uncle's handgun went off when it landed in the garbage can, and the bullet passed through Daniel's calf and out through the wall.

Painful as that injury was, Daniel Couch was lucky to limp away from this accident. However, many others aren't as lucky. Thousands of family members die every year because of improperly stored handguns. The solution to this problem is not to remove the handguns. The solution is to add one very simple safety feature that will keep handguns, even improperly stored handguns, from putting family members at risk: removable triggers.

In this two-paragraph opening, the first paragraph tells the anecdote, and the second paragraph transitions from that anecdote to an introduction of the topic and main idea. Spending this much time engaging the readers' interest makes this opening fairly informal. Your professors would be within their rights to complain, but as long as you don't go overboard with the anecdote, an opening like this can still be effective in a college essay.

This opening includes a thesis statement. It's the last sentence of the second paragraph. This sentence doesn't capture the full complexity of the essay's idea — that's the job of the *writerly* thesis statement — but it does briefly state the main point that the rest of the essay will explain and defend.

Textual References and Quotations

When your topic is a text of any sort, good manners and professional courtesy require you to introduce the author and title of the text early —

In Willa Cather's *My Ántonia*, the narrator . . .

Besides this obligatory introduction of the author and text, you must also guide your readers to your focus within this text — a quotation or passage or subtopic from the text that shows your readers what interests you — and what sort of idea they can expect from your essay. Here's an example:

In Willa Cather's *My Ántonia*, the narrator, Jim Burden, writes about every little thing he can remember. Looking back on his childhood experience of arriving on the Nebraska frontier in the middle of a moonless night, he writes: "There was nothing but land: not a country at all, but the material out of which countries are made.... Between that earth and that sky I felt erased, blotted out. I did not say my prayers that night: here, I felt, what would be would be." It's understandable that this would be a strong memory for a young boy, but would that boy be wrestling with the big questions of existence or simply trying to keep from falling out of the wagon? That leads us to a more important question: Just how far can we trust this narrator?

This sort of an essay might not be your cup of tea. Or you might prefer essays about *Jane Eyre*. However, the opening still does a good job of introducing the topic — the narrator of Willa Cather's novel — and it uses this passage to introduce a question about his reliability. You don't get a thesis statement, but you know you can expect an answer to that question.

Textual references aren't limited to essays about texts. They can be used with any topic. You might use them to illustrate an idea in the same way you would use an anecdote:

When Huck Finn finally gets some money at the end of Mark Twain's novel, *Huckleberry Finn*, he is able to handle civilization for about a month and it's time to "light out for the territories." He disappears from view, never to be seen again. In recent years, thousands have followed Huck Finn in his flight to the territories. These are young professionals who have amassed small fortunes as stockbrokers, software engineers, and baristas. Suddenly, they slip away to try to live more fulfilling lives in rural America. But here's a little secret: They won't ever find that elusive fulfillment in "the territories." Huck Finn never found it. Nobody does.

In this example, the quotation introduces the topic of escape — "lighting out for the territories." The writer then shows how this continues in current times and presents the main idea of the essay — that escape to "the territories" will not be fulfilling. The reference to *Huckleberry Finn* is only here to get us started. This will not be an essay about Twain's novel.

Provocative Statements

Another way to engage your readers is to start off with a line that seems untrue or that stirs up emotions for your readers. These provocative statements jolt your readers' brains into action. As long as you follow up with thoughtful discussion and appropriate information — and thus bring the readers around to your way of seeing things — this is an effective technique for openings. Here is an example of a short, provocative opening:

> Abortion is *not* murder. A fetus has no legal status as a human and thus cannot be murdered any more than a brain tumor can be murdered.

This gets the blood pumping, doesn't it? As long as this paragraph isn't simply baiting the readers — that is, stirring them up emotionally without delivering a thoughtful idea — something like this can be either an effective opening or the effective first lines of a longer opening.

Here's another provocative statement:

> It doesn't take a penis to be a man.

Okay, so what *does* it take to be a man? If you wonder how this writer will define manhood, and if you aren't offended by the use of the word "penis," then this is an effective first line of an opening. It also points out that any reference to body parts or bathroom duties — along with the use of off-color language — is risky business. Using shocking words merely to shock your readers is a bad policy, and it's been done so much that it's become a bit of a cliché, too. It almost always gets your readers' attention, but it's often the last thing that an offended reader sees before putting down the essay.

Other Techniques

In addition to these common techniques, you have a couple of other options that don't usually stand on their own as openings but may still be useful when used with other strategies.

Humor is not common in academic writing because academics are generally humorless. However, a *little* humor can still make be engaging, even if readers don't quite notice it. Good, thinks your biology instructor, not realizing that what she likes is that you introduce the topic of frog eggs by explaining that they have the texture and *taste* of gummy bears. In academic writing, a little humor goes a long way. Anything more doesn't go anywhere.

Questions are another useful device. If you ask your readers an interesting question, it arouses their curiosity. Just make sure you eventually answer any questions you raise — even if your answer is that this particular question has no easy answer. There's nothing worse than asking a great question and then denying your readers the satisfaction of a great response. That's like asking a friend, "You remember that twenty bucks I borrowed?" and then adding, "I still don't have it. Ha ha." It's not good for the relationship.

Are You Sure I Don't Need a Thesis Statement?

The old rule that you must have a thesis statement in the first paragraph is, like the five-paragraph trainer-essay that required it, too simple for more sophisticated essays.

You have less freedom with technical papers, scholarly research, and scientific papers. These almost always require an opening that includes a statement of what the essay will cover. That's because they are written for readers who are eager to read these papers but only if they contain the information or ideas they are looking for. Those science people hate to waste time. You will also have some professors who demand a thesis statement because it makes their job a lot easier.

However, unless you are bound by an academic discipline's formal expectations or the demands of a professor, it's your choice about whether or not to put a thesis statement in the opening. Your readers need to know what the topic and focus of the essay will be. They need to know what sort of idea to expect. One way to do that is to include a thesis statement and then let the body of the essay explain and defend that idea. But you can also ask a pointed question in the opening and let the body show readers how your information leads to a convincing answer. You have to decide what works best, essay by essay.

Write a Triumphant Closing

One good thing about writing the body first and the opening and closing later is that you might actually write a closing. When student writers start with the opening and then write the body, they often wear out by the end of the body. Having said all they really need to say in the body, they scribble down the barest of closings and quit. They become long-distance runners who sit down with ten yards to go and tell the cheering fans, "You get the point. I more or less ran the entire race."

Foolish student writers!

Are you tired? Take a nap. Then come back and tell your readers about the triumph that is the body of your essay. Remind them of your main points of information. Remind them about how those points work together to explain and defend your idea. And don't stop there. You should also give your readers something new as a parting gift — one final and engaging illustration that captures your main idea, or perhaps a few practical suggestions for what your readers can do with your idea.

Although you're right to think that the body of a good essay has said everything that needs to be said, your poor, distracted readers need more than that. Detailed information presents your idea clearly and effectively, but reading a lot of detailed information all at once can be taxing on a reader. It wears them out. To guide your readers through to the end of your essay, your closing has to summarize that information and briefly remind readers how it all adds up to explain your main idea. The closing should also emphasize that idea one last time.

The closing doesn't have to be long. It just has to be complete. Here's a single-paragraph closing that wraps things up effectively:

> Who then should bear the blame for this catastrophe? The evidence is clear enough. Shirley Roberts hired the uncertified electrician who installed the overhead lava lamps. Shirley Roberts never scheduled the electrical inspection that would have shown that the overhead lava lamps were defective and dangerous. Shirley Roberts removed the sprinkler system without any mention of this to her clients, even though she met with them fourteen times after this decision. Only one person is to blame for what happened on November 21: Shirley Roberts.

The repetition of the villain's name is the only writerly device the writer uses here. It reminds us of the topic of the essay. Otherwise, this is a simple summary of the main points of information from the body followed by an equally simple restatement of the main idea. That's long enough. It does its job.

If you want to wrap things up more colorfully, that's fine, too — as long as you still do the more important work of summarizing your information and emphasizing your main idea. You have many options for adding color to your closings, just as you have many options for openings. Anecdotes are popular. You can also bring in textual references and quotations. In addition to these favorites, you might try two other techniques that are only used with closings — the second half of an anecdote and the call to action.

The Second Half of an Anecdote

You set up this technique by telling the first half of an anecdote in the opening of your essay. That gives your readers some motivation to continue reading — to find out how the story ends. At the end of the essay, you reward them with the second half of the opening anecdote. Here is an example:

> What happened to Wild Bob? Unfortunately, Wild Bob's story ended like that of many others who suffer from TF. He lost his job because of the safety risks he posed. His family was driven away. Finally he gave up, sealed the air vents in his room, and let the disease run its course. Wild Bob's story illustrates how desperate life can be for victims of TF.
>
> As you've seen, however, ongoing research suggests that relief is on the way. Friesen and Friesen's identification of the TF gene is a step toward long-term eradication. Dr. Libby's research with monkey saliva builds on their efforts, opening the door to the genetic therapy proposed by Dylan in her groundbreaking paper. In the short term, the Beeler Foundation's "smelling nose" cats offer immediate help, as does the Coopers' creative use of water filtration technology. And let's not forget Richardson's astonishing results with therapeutic bowling, suggesting that a solution might be found with simple lifestyle changes.
>
> As this and other promising medical research suggests, we can soon write a new ending for the TF story. For that to happen, the research must move forward. This is why Congress must renew its funding for the TF Institute. The results of current work are too promising to be ignored. For all the Wild Bobs out there, continued funding is a matter of life and death.

This closing starts by giving readers some resolution with the sad ending of the Wild Bob anecdote. It follows that with a thorough summary of the information from the body. The last paragraph then connects both Wild

Bob and the summarized information to the main idea — keep the money coming because the research is making progress. This ending is a little long for a short essay. You don't want the closing to overshadow the body. However, it will work well with a longer, researched essay that has presented a lot of information.

The Call to Action

The call to action builds a bridge between the main idea and your readers by giving them practical ways to take the main idea and make it a part of their lives. If a call to action is appropriate for your main idea, it's a great closing because it makes your idea tangible for your readers. If they see how your idea connects to their lives, they understand it more clearly. The only weakness is that, on its own, a call to action doesn't summarize the details in the body and connect them to the main idea. That's easy to fix, though. You summarize the information first and then call your readers to action. Here's an example:

> Unfortunately, ending the practice of clear-cutting is more easily said than done. The majority of private forests are now held by huge timber corporations, and short-term profit is their primary goal. The majority of public forests are managed by government agencies that see our forests as agricultural crops. These factors make it challenging for the average person to influence forest practices directly. However, there are three easy, effective things to do to indirectly reduce or even remove clear-cutting as a widespread forest-management practice:
>
> 1. Use less timber. Buy recycled wood products such as OSB sheathing, HardiePlank siding, and decking made from plastic and recycled wood. These alternatives are becoming more common and can be found at most building supply stores.
>
> 2. Make your priorities known to your current elected representatives with letters and e-mails. They won't know you're unhappy unless you tell them, and they are savvy enough to know when the tide has finally turned.
>
> 3. Vote for politicians who care more about ecological forests than corporate profits. They are out there, and in increasing numbers.
>
> You can make a difference. You just have to take some first steps and encourage others to do the same. The rest will follow.

This is a lengthy closing, too, and again, that's okay as long as the body of the essay also takes its time laying out the details of its information. In this example, you have a writer who knows that the body of the essay is solid and is now taking a little victory lap.

Good for you, triumphant student writer!

The Big Ideas

Guiding your readers means going back to your essay and adding in a few simple ingredients that will help them to see how the information in the body of your essay works together to 1) explain your idea and 2) defend it. Your readers aren't stupid. They just don't know your thinking as well as you do. Here's what you can do to help:

1. Use topic sentences: They tell readers what to expect from each paragraph and they connect each paragraph to the topic or thesis of your essay. That's a lot.

2. Use transitions: Transitional sentences, phrases, and words point out organization and show readers how different ideas are related to each other.

3. Write an obvious opening: With formal writing, you tend to engage your readers by being obvious — telling them exactly what to expect so that they can see if this is the sort of thing they are looking for. So do that. But as long as you use restraint, you can jazz it up a little.

4. Write a triumphant closing: Don't just stop because you're tired. Suck it up and end with a flourish.

Chapter 12
Proofread Your Essay

After you have completed an essay for a class, you might be tempted to turn it in. Don't. It's not ready yet.

No way, you think. You feel good about this essay. It really flowed, and now you're ready to hand it in. Don't. You have one more very important task in front of you — proofreading.

Student writer, your sense of accomplishment is well earned. It's not easy to bring something new into the world, so it's kind of a big deal for you to know a topic well enough to have figured out an idea of your own. It's also a big deal that you have figured out how to explain that idea in an essay. That was a lot of work. A lot of personal investment of your time and intelligence. You *should* feel a sense of accomplishment when you write the last line of your triumphant closing.

However, your sense of accomplishment — up to this point — is merely personal. You feel good about what *you've* done, not about what your essay has done. And you don't really know what your essay's done because you haven't read it carefully yet. You've only seen it from your perspective as the writer. You haven't seen it from the perspective of your readers.

When it comes to judging the effectiveness of your essay, all that matters is what's on the page. The essay has to make sense on its own. To accurately judge whether your essay is really any good, then, you have to set aside your personal feelings and judge your essay the way that your readers will judge it — by actually reading it to see how well the words on the page do their job.

In this final chapter, we'll look at how to proofread your essay before you turn it in. You will have to ignore any feelings of accomplishment — or sense of dread. You will also have to leave yourself enough time at the end of the writing process to proofread. The main thing, though, is that you have to *decide* to proofread.

Proofread the Surface of the Essay

Proofreading focuses on the surface of the essay — word choice, sentence grammar, punctuation, formatting, and that sort of thing. That's because by this point in the writing process, the essay as a whole should be pretty good, with no major revision required to improve any weaknesses in thinking, information, organization, and so on.

If you *haven't* written a pretty good essay, proofreading won't do any damage, but it also won't miraculously transform a lousy essay into a good one. For that, you need to follow the three-step writing process, and you don't have time for that at this point. So keep that in mind for your next essay. Hopefully your writing professor has a generous revision policy with this one.

With that in mind, let's look at how to improve the surface.

Examine the Assignment Guidelines

The first thing to check is how well your essay matches the basic requirements of the assignment. I don't mean the topic or focus, though. It's too late to worry about that. I mean even more basic requirements. How long should the paper be? How should it be formatted? How does the professor want you to give credit to your sources — attribution or formal documentation?

Pay particular attention to the format of the essay. Appearances really matter. If your essay is formatted correctly, a lot of readers — including your professors — will assume that the essay is probably pretty good. I'm not joking. Careful readers will look beneath the surface to see if the essay is actually any good, but a good first impression goes a long way. Your readers are likely to give you the benefit of the doubt.

If the assignment requires formal documentation, it also requires the formatting rules for that documentation system, which includes margins, page numbering, allowable font sizes, and more. These rules are detailed and thorough, but it's nothing you can't handle. Just follow the documentation guidelines in your writing handbook or by searching online for the documentation style that's assigned (MLA, APA, and so on) and "formatting."

If the assignment requires no formal documentation, it's still a good idea to follow the formatting rules of a formal documentation system. That extra effort makes you look like a more serious student, even if you're not, and it makes your essay more readable. If you set your carefully formatted essay down next to the hand-written essay of another student, you'll see what I mean. So will the other, painfully envious student. *Awkward.*

> "If your essay is formatted correctly, a lot of readers — including your professors — will assume that the essay is probably pretty good. I'm not joking. Careful readers will look beneath the surface to see if the essay is actually any good, but a good first impression goes a long way."

Getting your formatting right will take a while at first, especially if you don't know how to use your word-processing software very well. However, you have many resources to help you with this. Any recent writing handbook will give you explanations and examples of how to format a paper. If you have access to a college writing center, the tutors there have been formatting papers since birth and will take pleasure in helping you format yours. The Internet is also filled with templates you can use and video guides to walk you through the process — all the good work of English graduate students building up their resumes before bravely entering the horrific reality of finding full-time work. And once you've figured it out, it won't take any extra time at all.

Your professor will often add other assignment requirements in addition to formatting. You might need to stay within minimum and maximum length requirements. You might need to use a minimum number of sources. Don't think of these rules as suggested guidelines. Think of them as felonies you'd rather not commit. Ignoring them shows your professor that you haven't taken the assignment seriously — not exactly the impression you want to make. So reread the assignment instructions to make sure you're following those guidelines. It will take two minutes. You have no excuse not to.

Examine the Sentences and Punctuation

The most prominent distractions in college writing are sentence-level mistakes with grammar, punctuation, word usage, and spelling. These are all errors that college writers are expected to avoid, and if they don't avoid them, they're judged somewhat harshly.

As for sentences, I understand, grammatically challenged student writer, that sentence grammar was originally taught when you were in fifth grade, and that the only thing you remember from fifth grade is the afternoon your sister Nadine busted you for smoking cigarettes in the garage. I also understand how unfair it is that now, after all those misspent years, you're expected to write grammatical sentences. So sad.

Unfortunately, gross unfairness doesn't change anything. It never does. You're now responsible for your sentences, and that's just the way it goes. Even if, after reading chapters 3 and 4 of this book, you struggle with grammatical sentences, you still have to proofread for sentence grammar, and as you do so, you have to keep developing your technical skills so that — *slowly* — it gets easier, so that you'll be able to write more clearly and confidently.

To examine sentences on your own, I'll again suggest the trick I mentioned in chapter 3 — read your paper backwards, sentence by sentence. That's awkward, and the reason is it *dis*organizes your paper. You strip away all the organization that would otherwise keep those sentences humming along as a unit in your mind. Every sentence now has to stand on its own — to make sense without the help of other sentences. Consider this somewhat cohesive group of sentences:

> Student writer, your sense of accomplishment is well earned. It's not easy to bring something new into the world, so it's kind of a big deal for you to know a topic well enough to have figured out an idea of your own. It's also a big deal that you have figured out how to explain that idea in an essay. That was a lot of work. A lot of personal investment of your time and intelligence. You *should* feel a sense of accomplishment when you write the last line of your triumphant closing.

Déjà vu! Anyway, as a unit, that set of sentences makes clear enough sense. Now read that same paragraph backwards, sentence by sentence:

1. You *should* feel a sense of accomplishment when you write the last line of your triumphant closing.

2. A lot of personal investment of your time and intelligence.

3. That was a lot of work.

4. It's also a big deal that you have figured out how to explain that idea in an essay.

5. It's not easy to bring something new into the world, so it's kind of a big deal for you to know a topic well enough to have figured out an idea of your own.

6. Student writer, your sense of accomplishment is well earned.

Do you see how #2 doesn't make as much sense anymore? That's because it's not a complete idea — not a grammatical sentence. It only makes sense if it follows #3, which tells you that #2 and #3 should probably be combined to create a sentence that includes both parts of this idea. Something like this:

> That was a lot of work and personal investment of your time and intelligence.

As you get more comfortable with the actual rules of grammar, you will understand why some sentences don't make sense. In this case, #2 didn't make sense because it was only a noun phrase. There was no predicate, so it was not a complete idea. However, even before you understand those grammar rules well enough to use them, you can still judge each of your sentences in this way to see if they make sense on their own. If they don't, you know that something has to be fixed.

A second thing to do to work on sentences is get professional help. That means getting sentence-level feedback from people with excellent grammar skills — English nerds of some sort. If you have a writing professor, ask your writing professor which grammar rules you should study first. If you don't have a writing professor but attend a school with a writing center, take your paper to the writing center and ask a writing center tutor for help with grammar. These people get red-faced and teary-eyed over the correct use of commas. They aren't great role models, but they're a great as a resource.

When it comes to punctuation, proofreading is a little more straight-forward. All you have to do is look at every single punctuation mark in your paper and ask yourself this simple question: "Why?" If the answer to that question is "I heard a pause" or "it felt right" or "I don't really know," then remove the punctuation mark and slap yourself on the forehead. Next, check to see whether a punctuation rule applies to the sentence. Look at the actual rules from chapter 4. If a rule applies to that sentence, then follow it. Add the punctuation mark. If a rule does not apply, then leave it out.

The main thing is that you stop guessing about punctuation and study the rules instead. They aren't that hard to figure out. And until you do have them figured out, only use punctuation when you *know* which rule requires it. It's usually less distracting to leave out necessary punctuation than to add unnecessary punctuation. That also helps your writing professor figure out which rules you need to learn next.

And finally, never — *never* — trust software to fix your sentences and punctuation. That's just asking for trouble. As you read in chapter 5, the spell-check software is simply guessing about spelling. Grammar-check software is even worse. It can't really tell if sentences are grammatical or not, so it makes stupid suggestions about punctuation.

Foolish grammar software!

Ignore its advice. Work on your own skills instead.

Examine the Words

Even if you have a great idea — and even if you explain that idea with excellent sentences — you can still drive readers away with unwise word choice.

My sister Nadine once told my mother to "get the hell out" of her bedroom. In the weeks of punishment that followed, Nadine complained that she had presented my mother with a reasonable idea. She had been preening in front of the mirror in her underwear when my mother barged in to ask where the vacuum cleaner had gone. Nadine, then in the bloom of a prolonged adolescence, had made an understandable request for privacy. Her idea might have been taken seriously if she had chosen her words more carefully. As it was, her word choice made her audience blind — as in, blind rage — to her idea.

We looked at this fairly closely in chapter 5, so I won't repeat that discussion here. However, I'll remind you about the three things to look at when it comes to words:

1. Choose the right word.

2. Spell your words correctly.

3. Be professional — not informal.

As a proofreader, the real challenge is to actually see the words with fresh — and somewhat fussy — eyes. We'll talk about that in the final section of this chapter.

Put Distance between You and Your Essay

As you can see, then, proofreading is the process of examining your own essay from the perspective of a fairly picky and unimpressed reader. You're looking at the surface of your paper, and you're looking for the problems, for the weaknesses. You're doing the same thing that my Uncle Larry does when he sits across from me at Thanksgiving and explains all the things I've done wrong — my absurd career choices, my snooty girlfriend or lack thereof, my receding hairline, my modest weight gain, my unconscionable failure to learn how to iron a dress shirt — *everything*. Happy Thanksgiving, Uncle Larry! That's the sort of mean-spirited scrutiny you need when proofreading.

And who wants to do that, right? It's bad enough when Uncle Larry gives you the Uncle Larry treatment. Why give the Uncle Larry treatment to yourself? You've been working on this paper for days, one would hope. You've researched your topic. You've thought about the evidence. You've carefully figured out and improved your main idea, planned your essay, and drafted it. And now I tell you to pick it apart? Now I tell you to tear it down?

Not exactly. I just want you to make a good essay even better. I want you to remove any errors from the surface of your essay so that your readers won't even notice the surface of your essay, so that all they see is your thoughtful main idea and all those glittering details. And I don't want you to give *you* the Uncle Larry treatment, either. I want you to give your *essay* the Uncle Larry treatment. There's a big difference.

As I've already told you, what you've written is just that — something you've written. It's not you. It's not a measure of your intelligence. It's just an essay, and if it measures anything, it measures is your skills as a writer *at this moment*. It's better than your essays used to be, and it's worse than your essays will be in the future. So that's what gets the Uncle Larry treatment — the thing that you made, not you.

And that's where you find the real challenge of proofreading. After you've put so much time into creating your essay, the final product is so much a part of your thinking that it's hard to see what's on the page. For you, the essay exists as all those facts and ideas in your brain *and* as the actual words on the page. If anything is missing on the page, no problem! Your brain still remembers all the facts and ideas that your paper forgot to explain, so it pretends they made it to the page.

To give your essay the Uncle Larry treatment, you have to put some distance between you and your essay. You have to step away from your brain and focus only on the words that have actually made it to the page. You have to see your essay as just a collection of words — words that might have been written by anyone.

Putting distance between you and your essay is not easy. Even professional writers, people whose livelihoods depend on the effective use of words, have a hard time separating themselves from the things they have written. However, there are a number of practices and resources available that will help make the proofreading process more successful. And the more proofreading you do, the easier that process will become.

If you have a writing professor, for example, your professor can help you see your essay with new eyes. You will get comments from your professor after the paper is turned in, so don't dread them. Don't avoid them. Don't avert your eyes. You paid good money for those comments, so pay attention to them. Read them closely. Turn to your professor and thank him for taking the time to give this detailed feedback. And be sincere about it, too. Those comments will help you learn how to see essays for what they are — that they are not you.

You can also ask your professor for feedback on the essay before you turn in a final draft. That will help you to proofread and improve your essay in advance of the deadline. Just make sure that this happens well before the paper's deadline. Don't show up early to class and ask for quick pointers on how to make the paper get an A in the five minutes before you turn it in. That will give your professor something to smile about, but that's all you'll get.

If you attend a school with a writing center, use that excellent resource to put some distance between you and your essay. Those writing center tutors will be happy to give it the Uncle Larry treatment. And as you listen to them, you'll also begin to see how they look at essays. It's probably not how you look at essays yet, but it's how you should start looking at formal writing if you want your work to be professional and effective.

> "To give your essay the Uncle Larry treatment, you have to put some distance between you and your essay.... You have to see your essay as just a collection of words — words that might have been written by anyone."

If you don't have access to a writing professor or writing center, you might have access to others who have at least *some* background with formal writing. These might be relatives who were English majors before they entered their present careers in food service. They might be friends who have done well in writing classes — or who are just hard to please. As long as these readers are willing to be honest about what's confusing or distracting, they can help you to put some distance between you and your essay.

But be careful about using friends and relatives. Don't get mad if they tell you there are problems. When you do that, you end up missing the problems and losing them as future readers. Just keep thanking them for the observations. Buy them pizza, babysit their kids, rub their tired feet. You need to honor their efforts to help you with your word choice because careful reading is not the easiest thing to do.

When you're writing an essay for a class, you have access to other students who are also writing essays for that class. In some cases, your professor will require you to share your essay with those students, to offer and receive feedback. Make the most of that sometimes awkward opportunity by making your essay as good as possible before you share it. That way, anything useful you hear from other students will be something you haven't figured out on your own. It will help you to make the essay better than you could have made it by yourself.

> **"In some cases, your professor will require you to share your essay with those students.... Make the most of that sometimes awkward opportunity by making your essay as good as possible before you share it."**

Second, pay attention to what they say. Keep your mouth shut and listen. Your colleagues might not be able to explain themselves very well — they're still just students, after all, like you — but they can still identify the places in your essay that were confusing, and that will help you to take a look at the essay through their eyes.

One thing you can do on your own is to use time to create some distance between you and your essay. Finish the essay a day or two before the deadline and set it aside. Then come back to the essay and see what you think. You'll be amazed. It won't be the same essay. Your brain will have moved on to other challenges, so if you left out the word "not," you'll notice that now. If you used "coma" instead of "comma," you'll see that now and be able to fix it. Time is great for creating distance. The only problem is creating the time in the first place.

If you don't have a day or two to let the essay cool off, have someone read your paper to you. This is where you can use friends and family who have no idea how formal writing works. All they have to do is read your essay out loud. When they read the paper to you, it puts you in the place of the reader by turning your essay into a spoken thing that exists entirely outside of your brain. It also helps identify sentences that don't make sense. Whenever your reader stumbles, stop the reader and check the sentence.

And if you have no one around who is willing to read your essay to you, you can read it out loud to yourself. That's not as effective — your brain will still try to smooth over the problems — but it's better than reading it silently. It makes it harder for your brain to trick you into thinking that the essay is good to go when it's not.

Keep Proofreading in Its Place

One last thing to remember about proofreading is that it should be the last thing you do with your essay before you print it on clean white paper and put a staple through the upper left corner.

If you start proofreading and revising your essay while you're still drafting it, there's a good chance that you will freeze up with anxiety and never finish that draft. It's easy to write and rewrite and tinker with the first paragraph for so long that the second paragraph withers from neglect and eventually dies a quiet death. It's also easy to get so freaked out by punctuation and sentence grammar that you stop making sentences entirely.

Don't give your essay the Uncle Larry treatment too soon. Rough drafts are rough for a reason. Let them be rough so that they can get drafted. You should only start proofreading after all of the ideas and information in your brain have been converted into words on the page. In fact, you should only start after you have written and *revised* your essay.

As a proofreader, you're not rewriting the essay anymore. At this point, you're only trying to take a good thing and make it better. You're brushing the teeth of your essay to freshen its breath and to remove any parsley that got stuck in its smile. This is important work because you want to make a good impression. You don't want any distractions to get in the way of your essay's ideas. However, it's still superficial work. Most of your time should go into educating yourself, finding a good main idea, and then using detailed information to explain and defend that idea.

If proofreading leads you to the chilling realization that what you've written is not, in fact, a good or appropriate essay for an assignment, don't panic or despair. This is just an essay, after all. It has its place in the universe, but it's not a very big place. What matters more is what you do with this chilling realization. You need to see it for what it is — a sign that you could have done better, and that you know you could have done better. You're getting somewhere, student writer. You're learning what to expect of yourself. Go ahead and turn in that essay, such as it is, and then, when you write your next essay, do the better work that you know you're capable of.

And you will do better work, too. This is just writing after all, and anyone who keeps on writing learns how to write better.

The Big Ideas

Proofreading means going back to your almost-finished essay and cleaning up anything that might distract readers from your otherwise brilliant thinking and writing. Keep these ideas in mind:

1. All that matters is what's on the page: To judge whether your essay is really any good, you have to judge your essay the way that your readers will judge it — by actually reading it and testing whether the words on the page do their job.

2. Proofreading focuses on the surface of the essay: That includes word choice, sentence grammar, formal punctuation, formatting, and so on. If the main idea and evidence aren't very good, proofreading won't help make the essay much better, but it won't hurt, either.

3. Put some distance between yourself and your essay: If you're on your own, time is the best way to put distance between you and your essay. However, there are many other ways to get some distance, such as reading the essay out loud and getting feedback from others.

4. Keep proofreading in its place: Only proofread after the essay is otherwise finished. If you start polishing a paragraph before the rest of the essay is written, the rest of the essay becomes harder to write.

Conclusion
Now What?

Now you write.

If you've made it this far — and apparently you have — you've learned a lot of new ideas about formal writing. You've seen what formal readers expect from you, things like sticking to one idea, building formal paragraphs, using grammatical sentences, and choosing words carefully. You've also learned about a writing process in which you spend most of your time educating yourself and figuring out a good idea. Only then do you turn to the task of explaining yourself with a detailed, organized explanation of your idea. That's a lot to absorb.

So absorb. Soak it up. Put these ideas into practice so that they become a natural part of how you write — so that you become a decent formal writer. If you've read this book as part of a writing class, you have a good start on the absorption process because your writing professor kept you writing formal papers all term long. That's helped you to see for yourself what it means to write in a more formal way. But sure to say thank you on your way out the door.

But remember that a writing class is just a starting point. It's like you learning how to drive with a student permit while an anxious adult sits beside you the passenger seat telling you to speed up, to use your turn signal, and to tap on your brakes — tap on them *now*. To really become an effective writer, you have to keep writing in this way to until you become comfortable and then confident with formal writing. Until you can do it on your own, in other words.

So when you're assigned to write your next paper in biology or world history or American literature, don't go back to your old habits as an informal writer. Write a formal paper. Take the time to educate yourself. Take the time to find and improve a good main idea. Take the time to present that idea carefully. And maybe even take your paper to your college writing center to get some feedback before you turn it in. This is where you will really make the leap forward, when you're writing on your own and don't have a writing professor telling you what to do all the time.

And there will be other opportunities for you to write formally, too. You'll apply for jobs and scholarships. You'll apply for internships or admission to other schools. You might drop out of college because you're a genius of some sort, but even then you'll need to get financing so you can create the next big thing and become a bajillionaire. For that, you'll need to write proposals, overviews, and business plans. In all of these situations, the same ideas apply. Do your research. Think about what you need to say. Carefully plan, draft, and revise your paper.

And while you probably don't need to invest as much time in your informal writing, it's still a good idea for you to practice these ideas with your e-mail and notes and letters to well-off, elderly relatives. Think about what you're trying to do. Think about how best to do that. Explain yourself with plenty of details. Choose your words carefully. Be organized. That will make your informal writing more effective, too.

When my sister Nadine got her driver's license, that license seemed to tell her that she was now a fully developed driver with nothing more to learn. But her driver's license was lying. She was *not* a fully developed driver. She was an occasionally adequate driver who had much, much more to learn about how to drive safely and considerately on public roads. But because she thought she was done learning how to drive, she actually was done learning how to drive.

And I'll be honest, Nadine is a *terrible* driver. To this day, it's simply not safe to be in or near a car that she is driving. She rear-ends someone about once a year. Never pays attention to speed limits. Changes lanes without looking. Runs stop signs. Talks on her cell phone. She once tried to park her car in a parking space that was occupied by another car. But if you make the mistake of telling Nadine that she's a terrible driver, she will gladly let you know that you are an idiot because she has been a licensed driver for more than twenty years. It's actually been more than thirty years, but she likes to leave the impression that she is younger than she is.

That same sort of thing could happen to you if you get the wrong-headed idea that taking a writing class or reading a book is what makes you a good writer. You become a good writer when you begin to write well, and that only happens with practice.

So for the time being, continue to think of yourself as a student writer, student writer. Continue to practice these ideas and improve your skills. It probably won't take long before the "student" part drops off and you find that you really are a good writer, comfortable with the rules of formal writing and confident in your abilities to put your ideas into words. But until that happens, assume that you could use a little more practice — because you probably could.

And listen, if you're out driving and happen to notice a maroon Buick LeSabre swerving from side to side behind you, trying to pass, there's a good chance that it's Nadine. My advice is to pull over and let her pass. She *will* pass you, one way or another, so it's best to just get out of her way.

CPSIA information can be obtained
at www.ICGtesting.com
Printed in the USA
LVOW01s2231280816
502209LV00021B/265/P